Math Skills

Grade 4

Adapted from Steck-Vaughn Working with Numbers, Level D

Illustrator: Rebecca Elliot

ISBN: 978-1-4114-0109-9

Please submit all inquiries to FlashKids@bn.com

Printed and bound in Canada

Lot #:

22 24 25 23

06/13

Flash Kids
A Division of Barnes & Noble
122 Fifth Avenue
New York, NY 10011

Dear Parent,

As you bring math learning into your home, you are helping your child to strengthen the skills that he or she is taught in the classroom. Your efforts also emphasize how math is useful outside of school, as well as necessary for success in everyday life.

To assist you, this colorful, fun workbook presents grade-appropriate math concepts and language to your child in a way that is logical and organized. Each section begins with clear examples that illustrate new skills, and then practice drills, problem-solving lessons, and unit reviews encourage your child to master each new technique.

This Grade 4–level workbook begins with exercises in estimation that reinforce your child's ability to calculate sums and differences. Unit 2 emphasizes the multiplication skills that were featured in Grade 3, and then Units 3, 4, and 5 thoroughly develop these skills, teaching your child techniques to solve complex multiplication and division problems. Next, using time, money, and measurement, Unit 6 introduces problems requiring conversion, which is then applied to basic fractions and geometry in Unit 7.

As you and your child work through each unit, try to show your child how to apply each skill in everyday situations. For example, at the grocery store you can ask your child to guess, and then determine exactly, how many $0.75/lb. apples you can purchase with six one-dollar bills. This exercise requires your child to apply many different math skills to a single, real-life problem. As your child draws connections between concepts presented separately in this workbook, he or she learns to reason mathematically, an ability critical for success through future years of math instruction.

Also, consider how you can turn the following activities into fun math exercises for you and your child to do together:

- Identifying geometric shapes and angles of objects spotted during car trips;
- Purchasing enough food and drinks for a family dinner or a party;
- Rolling coins to exchange for paper money;
- Calculating how much material needed to make new curtains, build bookshelves, or carpet a room;
- Determining how much time left before the next planned activity of the day;
- Measuring ingredients to be used in cooking, and if necessary, dividing amounts to adjust the recipe.

Use your imagination! With help from you and this workbook, your child is well on the way to math proficiency.

Table of Contents

unit 1

Working with Whole Numbers

Place Value to Thousands	6
Place Value to Millions	7
Reading and Writing Numbers	8
Comparing Whole Numbers	9
Problem-Solving Method: Use Logic	10–11
Problem-Solving	12
Addition: Basic Facts	13
Addition	14
Regrouping in Addition	15
Addition of Three Numbers	16
Subtraction: Basic Facts	17
Subtraction	18
Regrouping in Subtraction	19
Regrouping Twice in Subtraction	20
Addition and Subtraction	21
Estimation by Rounding Numbers	22
Estimation of Sums	23
Estimation of Differences	24
Problem-Solving Method: Identify Extra Information	25–26
Unit 1 Review	27–29

unit 2

Multiplication and Division Facts

Multiplication Facts Through 5	30
Multiplication Facts for 6 and 7	31
Multiplication Facts for 8 and 9	32
Multiplication Table	33
Problem-Solving Method: Make a Model	34–35
Division Facts Through 5	36
Division Facts for 6 and 7	37
Division Facts for 8 and 9	38
Problem-Solving Method: Choose an Operation	39–40
Unit 2 Review	41–43

unit 3

Multiplying by One-digit Numbers

Multiplying by One-digit Numbers to 5	44–45
Multiplying by One-digit Numbers with Regrouping	46
Multiplying Numbers with Zeros by One-digit Numbers	47
Problem-Solving Method: Use Estimation	48–49
Multiplying by 6 and 7	50
Multiplying by 8 and 9	51
Problem-Solving Method: Solve Multi-Step Problems	52–53
Unit 3 Review	54–55

unit 4

Dividing by One-digit Numbers

Dividing Two-digit Numbers by 2, 3, 4, and 5	56
Dividing Three-digit Numbers by 2, 3, 4, and 5	57
Dividing with Remainders	58–59
Problem-Solving Method: Use Guess and Check	60–61
Dividing by 6 and 7	62
Dividing by 8 and 9	63
Problem-Solving Method: Write a Number Sentence	64–65
Unit 4 Review	66–67

unit 5

Multiplying and Dividing Larger Numbers

Multiplying by Tens and Hundreds	68–69
Multiplying Two-digit Numbers by Two-digit Numbers	70–71
Multiplying Three-digit Numbers by Two-digit Numbers	72–73
Estimating Products	74–75
Problem-Solving Method: Make a Table	76–77
Dividing by 10	78
Dividing by Tens	79
Zeros in Quotients	80–81
Trial Quotients: Too Large	82
Trial Quotients: Too Small	83
Two-digit Divisors	84–85
Estimating Quotients	86–87
Problem-Solving Method: Complete a Pattern	88–89
Problem-Solving	90
Unit 5 Review	91–93

unit 6

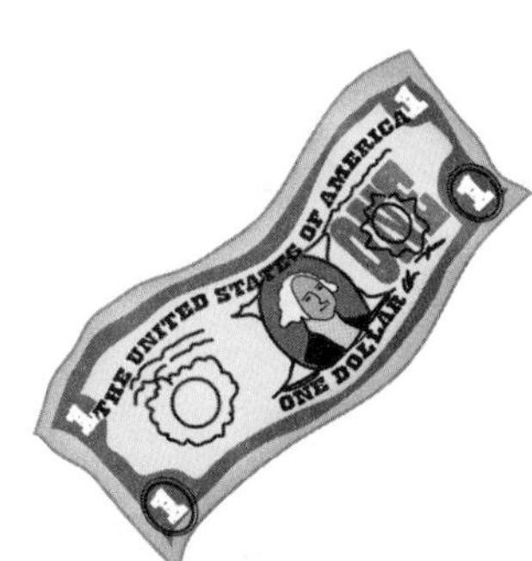

Time, Money, and Measurement

Time	94
Calendar	95
Elapsed Time	96
Using a Schedule	97
Money	98
Add and Subtract Money	99
Multiply and Divide Money	100
Problem-Solving Method: Work Backwards	101–102
Customary Units	103
Metric Units	104
Comparing Units of Measurement	105
Problem-Solving Method: Use a Graph	106–107
Unit 6 Review	108–109

unit 7

Fractions and Geometry

Meaning of Fractions	110
Using Fractions	111
Adding Fractions	112
Subtracting Fractions	113
Problem-Solving Method: Make an Organized List	114–115
Plotting Points on a Coordinate Grid	116
Lines, Rays, and Line Segments	117
Exploring Angles	118
Perimeter	119
Area	120
Problem-Solving Method: Use a Formula	121–122
Unit 7 Review	123–124
Answer Key	125–128

unit 1
working with whole numbers

Place Value to Thousands

Every **whole number** with four **digits** has a thousands, hundreds, tens, and ones place.

Th	H	T	O	Number
5,	7	4	6	= *5,746*

5 is in the thousands place. Its value is 5,000.		7 is in the hundreds place. Its value is 700.		4 is in the tens place. Its value is 40.		6 is in the ones place. Its value is 6.		
5,000	+	700	+	40	+	6	=	5,746

Write each number.

	a	*b*	*c*
1.	Th H T O: 2, 5 6 1 = *2,561*	Th H T O: 4, 7 3 9 = ______	Th H T O: 6, 2 6 8 = ______
2.	Th H T O: 8, 0 9 1 = ______	Th H T O: 5, 4 7 3 = ______	Th H T O: 3, 5 0 2 = ______
3.	Th H T O: 6, 6 4 8 = ______	Th H T O: 9, 7 2 2 = ______	Th H T O: 2, 0 5 9 = ______
4.	Th H T O: 3, 5 4 1 = ______	Th H T O: 1, 9 4 3 = ______	Th H T O: 5, 5 4 0 = ______

Write each number.

5. 7 thousands 4 hundreds 5 tens 2 ones = *7,452*

6. 3 thousands 0 hundreds 9 tens 5 ones = ______

7. 8 thousands 6 hundreds 2 tens 0 ones = ______

Write the value of each underlined digit.

	a		*b*		*c*	
8.	8,$\underline{6}$94	*600*	$\underline{6}$,324	______	7,90$\underline{4}$	______
9.	5,0$\underline{3}$9	______	7,$\underline{3}$34	______	$\underline{9}$58	______
10.	$\underline{8}$,694	______	$\underline{6}$,157	______	8,90$\underline{4}$	______

Place Value to Millions

A **place-value chart** can help you understand whole numbers. Each digit in a number has a value based on its place in the number.

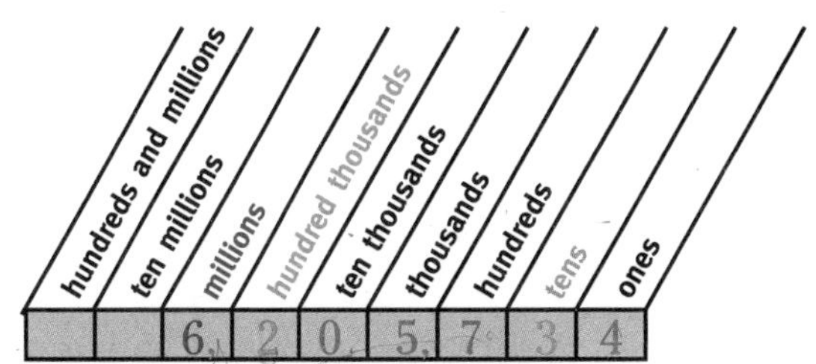

The 6 is in the millions place.
Its value is 6 millions or 6,000,000.
The 2 is in the hundred-thousands place.
Its value is 2 hundred thousands or 200,000.
The 3 is in the tens place.
Its value is 3 tens or 30.

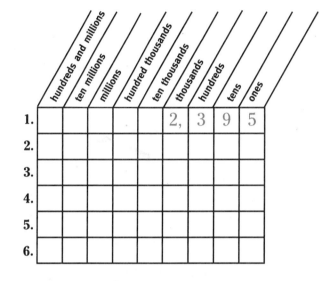

Write each number in the place-value chart.

1. 2,395
2. 418,702
3. 20,091,576
4. 987
5. 13,820
6. 5,482,637

	hundreds and millions	ten millions	millions	hundred thousands	ten thousands	thousands	hundreds	tens	ones
1.						2,	3	9	5
2.									
3.									
4.									
5.									
6.									

Write the place name for the 4 in each number.

	a		*b*
7. 251,349	tens	1,147,865	Ten thousand
8. 104,361,870	millon	51,428	hunderds
9. 1,264	one's	49,617,501	Ten millon
10. 8,504,976	thousand	439,060	hundreds

Write the value of the underlined digit.

	a		*b*
11. 121,764	7 hundreds or 700	283,145,167	
12. 56,340	0 ones or 0	2,401,637	
13. 3,412,906	3 millon or 3,000,000	892,465,182	
14. 196,358		410,295	

Reading and Writing Numbers

We read and write the number in this place-value chart as: twelve thousand, forty-five.

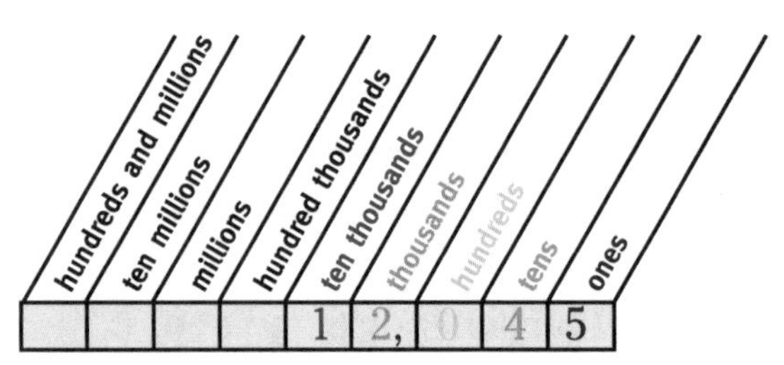

The digit 1 means 1 ten thousand, or 10,000.
The digit 2 means 2 thousands, or 2,000.
The digit 0 means 0 hundreds, or 0.
The digit 4 means 4 tens, or 40.
The digit 5 means 5 ones, or 5.

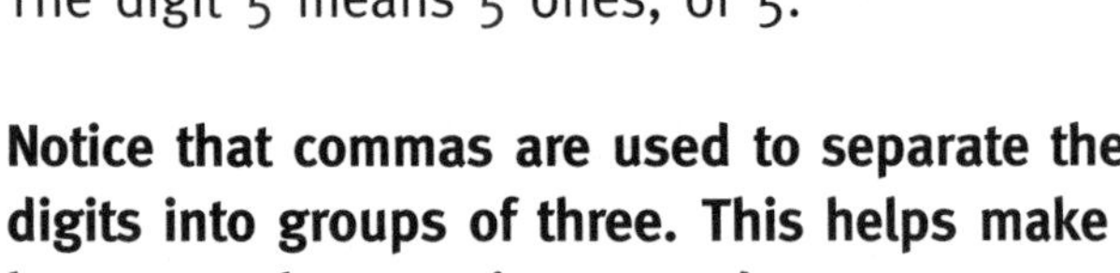

Notice that commas are used to separate the digits into groups of three. This helps make larger numbers easier to read.

Rewrite each number. Insert commas where needed.

	a	b	c
1.	345156 *345,156*	10105 ______	221689 ______
2.	2970534 ______	369571 ______	50148 ______
3.	17652017 ______	5304602 ______	189360 ______

Write each number using digits. Insert commas where needed.

4. five hundred twenty-nine thousand, thirty-one *529,031*

5. seventy-six thousand, four hundred eleven ______

6. eight million, fifty thousand, two hundred ______

7. two thousand, three hundred seven ______

8. ninety-four thousand, six hundred fifty-five ______

Write each number using words. Insert commas where needed.

9. 23,880 *twenty-three thousand, eight hundred eighty*

10. 730,604 ______

11. 19,042 ______

12. 5,208,000 ______

Comparing Whole Numbers

To compare two numbers, begin at the left.
Compare the digits in each place.

The symbol $<$ means **is less than.** $3 < 4$
The symbol $>$ means **is greater than.** $8 > 6$
The symbol $=$ means **is equal to.** $7 = 7$

Compare 47 and 29.

4 7
2 9

$4 > 2$, so $47 > 29$.

Compare 123 and 98.

1 2 3
0 9 8

$1 > 0$, so $123 > 98$.

Compare 326 and 351.

3 2 6
3 5 1

The hundreds digits are the same. Compare the tens digits.

$2 < 5$, so $326 < 351$.

Compare. Write $<$, $>$, or $=$.

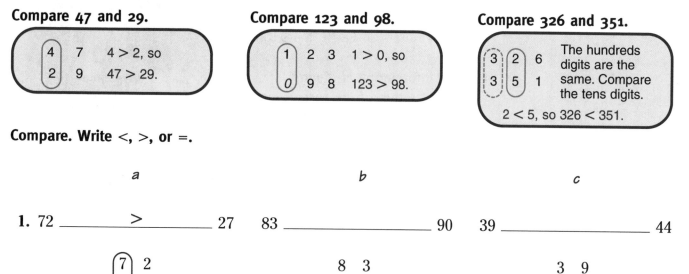

	a	b	c
1.	72 ____ $>$ ____ 27 7 2 2 7	83 ________ 90 8 3 9 0	39 ________ 44 3 9 4 4
2.	58 ________ 59 5 8 5 9	563 ________ 356 5 6 3 3 5 6	721 ________ 712 7 2 1 7 1 2
3.	619 ________ 640	468 ________ 468	226 ________ 220
4.	893 ________ 98	3,695 ________ 3,659	7,291 ________ 7,921
5.	35 ________ 35	62 ________ 92	100 ________ 99
6.	207 ________ 204	380 ________ 80	174 ________ 474

Problem-Solving Method: Use Logic

Mars and Venus are the closest planets to Earth. The **diameter,** or distance, across one of these three planets is 7,520 miles. The diameters of the other two planets are 4,222 miles and 7,926 miles. Mars is less than 7,000 miles across. Earth is larger than Venus. What are the diameters of Earth, Mars, and Venus?

Understand the problem.

- **What do you want to know?**
  the diameters of Earth, Mars, and Venus

- **What information is given?**
  The diameters of the three planets are 7,520, 4,222, and 7,926 miles.
  Clue 1: Mars is less than 7,000 miles across.
  Clue 2: Earth is larger than Venus.

Plan how to solve it.

- **What method can you use?**
  You can use logic to find all the possibilities. Then you can organize the information in a table.

	7,520 miles	4,222 miles	7,926 miles
Mars	no	**YES**	no
Venus	**YES**	no	no
Earth	no	no	**YES**

Solve it.

- **How can you use this method to solve the problem?**
  Since each planet has one diameter measurement, there can only be one YES in each row and column. Use the clues in the problem to fill out the table.

- **What is the answer?**
  The diameter of Earth is 7,926 miles.
  The diameter of Mars is 4,222 miles.
  The diameter of Venus is 7,520 miles.

Look back and check your answer.

- **Is your answer reasonable?**
  Clue 1: Mars is less than 7,000 miles across.
  Check: 4,222 < 7,000
  Clue 2: Earth is larger than Venus.
  Check: 7,926 > 7,520

The answer matches the clues.
The answer is reasonable.

Use logic to solve each problem.

1. The three largest sharks in the world are the great white, basking, and whale shark. Their weights are 7,300 pounds, 46,297 pounds, and 32,000 pounds. Great whites are not the largest. Basking sharks weigh less than 30,000 pounds. How much does a great white shark weigh?

Clue 1: Great whites are not the largest.

Clue 2: Basking sharks weigh less than 30,000 pounds.

great white shark ______________

	7,300	46,297	32,000
White			
Basking			
Whale			

2. Wilt Chamberlain, Michael Jordan, and Kareem Abdul-Jabbar scored the most points in the NBA. Their records are 29,277 points, 38,387 points, and 31,419 points. Chamberlain scored more points than Jordan. Abdul-Jabbar scored more than 31,500 points. What are Chamberlain's, Jordan's, and Abdul-Jabbar's scoring records?

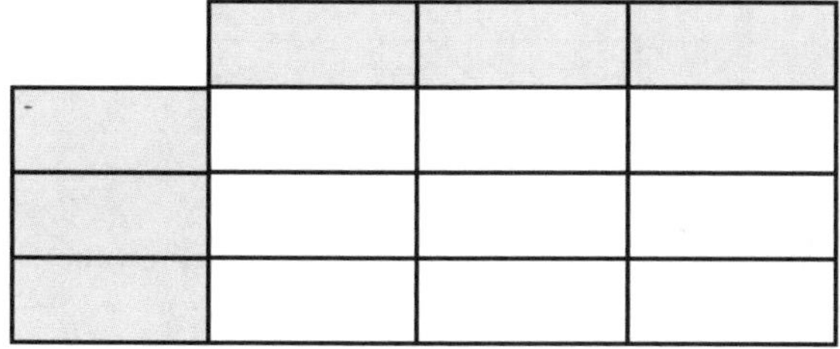

Chamberlain ______________

Jordan ______________

Abdul-Jabbar ______________

3. The "Beast," "Shivering Timbers," and "Mean Streak" are the world's longest wooden roller coasters. The longest is 7,400 feet. The other two are 5,384 feet and 5,427 feet long. "Mean Streak" is not the longest. The length of "Shivering Timbers" does not have a 4 in the hundreds place. How long is each roller coaster?

"Beast" ______________

"Shivering Timbers" ______________

"Mean Streak" ______________

Problem Solving

Write each number using words.

1. With a diameter of 88,840 miles, Jupiter is is the largest planet in our solar system.

   Answer ______________________________

   ____

2. *Titanic* was one of the most expensive movies ever made. It cost $250,000,000.

   Answer ______________________________

   ____

Write each number using digits.

3. Most people blink their eyes nine thousand, three hundred sixty-five times a day.

   Answer ______________________________

4. The world's biggest ice cream sundae was made in 1988. It weighed forty-five thousand, one hundred eighty pounds.

   Answer ______________________________

Compare. Write the greater number using digits.

5. A lion can weigh five hundred fifty-one pounds. A tiger can weigh six hundred sixty-one pounds.

   Answer ______________________________

6. The Nile River is four thousand, one hundred forty-five miles long. The Amazon River is four thousand, seven miles long.

   Answer ______________________________

Compare. Write the lesser number using words.

7. The average person in Japan watches 3,285 hours of television each year. The average person in the United States watches 2,555 hours each year.

   Answer ______________________________

   ____

8. Yankee Stadium in New York can seat 55,070 people. Dodger Stadium in California can seat 56,000 people.

   Answer ______________________________

   ____

Addition: Basic Facts

Add two numbers to find a **sum** or total.

Remember,

- adding 3 + 6 is the same as adding 6 + 3.
- adding 4 + 8 is the same as finding the sum of 4 and 8.

Add.

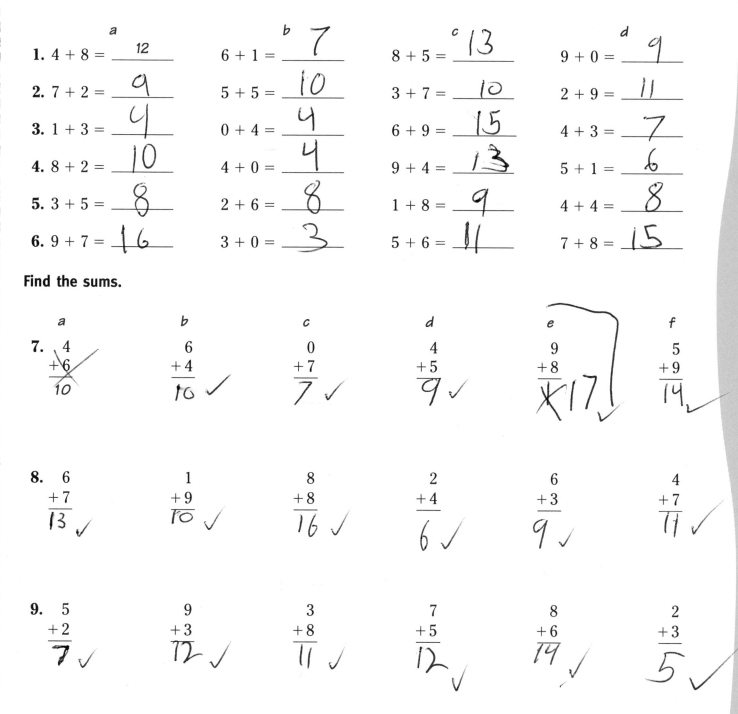

	a	b	c	d
1.	4 + 8 = 12	6 + 1 = ____	8 + 5 = ____	9 + 0 = ____
2.	7 + 2 = ____	5 + 5 = ____	3 + 7 = ____	2 + 9 = ____
3.	1 + 3 = ____	0 + 4 = ____	6 + 9 = ____	4 + 3 = ____
4.	8 + 2 = ____	4 + 0 = ____	9 + 4 = ____	5 + 1 = ____
5.	3 + 5 = ____	2 + 6 = ____	1 + 8 = ____	4 + 4 = ____
6.	9 + 7 = ____	3 + 0 = ____	5 + 6 = ____	7 + 8 = ____

Find the sums.

	a	b	c	d	e	f
7.	4 +6 10	6 +4	0 +7	4 +5	9 +8	5 +9
8.	6 +7	1 +9	8 +8	2 +4	6 +3	4 +7
9.	5 +2	9 +3	3 +8	7 +5	8 +6	2 +3

Addition

To add larger numbers, start with the digits in the ones place.

Find: 524 + 163

Add the ones.	Add the tens.	Add the hundreds.
H T O 5 2 **4** +1 6 **3** _ _ 7	H T O 5 **2** 4 +1 **6** 3 _ 8 7	H T O **5** 2 4 +**1** 6 3 6 8 7

Add.

	a	*b*	*c*	*d*	*e*
1.	T O 2 5 + 4 2 9	T O 4 6 + 3	T O 8 0 + 9	T O 5 +6 3	T O 9 2 + 7
2.	2 3 +3 4	5 3 +4 2	3 4 +5 5	4 0 +5 0	1 6 +7 3
3.	1 4 1 +8 2 0	4 0 0 +2 5 3	4 2 0 +3 0 7	3 6 0 +6 0 8	5 1 7 +1 6 2
4.	1 2 5 + 3 3	6 5 4 +2 2 5	1 2 +7 4 2	2 0 0 + 9 0	1 7 +5 4 2

Line up the digits. Then find the sums.

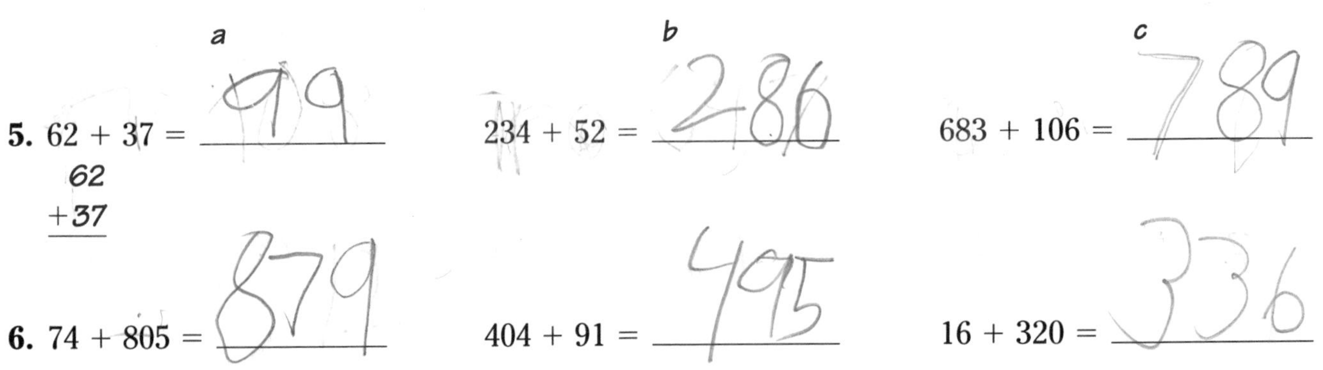

	a	*b*	*c*
5.	62 + 37 = ______ 62 +37	234 + 52 = ______	683 + 106 = ______
6.	74 + 805 = ______	404 + 91 = ______	16 + 320 = ______

Regrouping in Addition

Add the ones first. **Regroup** when there are ten or more.

Find: 864 + 456

Add the ones.
4 + 6 = 10 ones

	Th	H	T	O
			1	
		8	6	**4**
+		4	5	**6**
				0

Regroup:
10 ones =
1 ten
0 ones

Add the tens.
1 + 6 + 5 = 12 tens

	Th	H	T	O
		1	1	
		8	**6**	4
+		4	**5**	6
			2	0

Regroup:
12 tens =
1 hundred
2 tens

Add the hundreds.
1 + 8 + 4 = 13 hundreds

	Th	H	T	O
		1	1	
		8	6	4
+		**4**	5	6
	1,	3	2	0

Regroup:
13 hundreds =
1 thousand
3 hundreds

Add.

	a	b	c	d	e
1.	T|O	T|O	T|O	T|O	T|O
	1				
	3|6	2|9	3|5	4|4	2|6
	+4|5	+3|2	+1|9	+1|8	+2|7
	8|1				

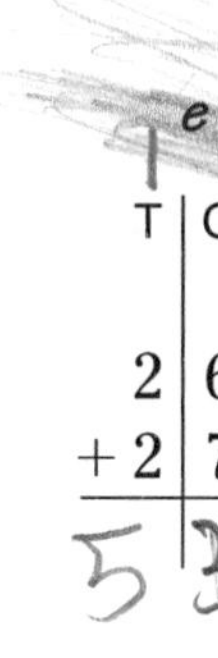

	a	b	c	d	e
	1 1				
2.	49	58	74	83	49
	+73	+66	+48	+49	+84
	122				
	1				
3.	457	608	49	853	36
	+ 28	+ 49	+490	+ 39	+382
	485				
	1 1 1				
4.	936	795	984	827	475
	+487	+325	+326	+496	+715
	1,423				

Line up the digits. Then find the sums.

5. a. 32 + 29 = ______________ b. 734 + 329 = ______________ c. 347 + 82 = ______________

32
+29

Addition of Three Numbers

To add three numbers, use the same steps as when adding two numbers. Regroup as needed.

Find: 354 + 683 + 95

Add the ones. Regroup.

	Th	H	T	O
			1	
		3	5	4
		6	8	3
+			9	5
				2

Add the tens. Regroup.

	Th	H	T	O
		2	1	
		3	5	4
		6	8	3
+			9	5
			3	2

Add the hundreds. Regroup.

	Th	H	T	O
		2	1	
		3	5	4
		6	8	3
+			9	5
	1,	1	3	2

Add.

	a	b	c	d	e
1.	H T O 1 75 20 +38 133	T O 36 14 +86	T O 90 8 +35	T O 87 66 + 2	T O 46 92 +38
2.	495 830 +185	276 53 +197	562 173 + 34	332 486 +200	631 293 +380
3.	192 706 + 58	440 178 +509	393 64 +270	54 317 +800	575 428 +358

Line up the digits. Then find the sums.

4. *a* 45 + 29 + 732 = ________

  45
  29
+732

b 457 + 234 + 158 = ________

Subtraction: Basic Facts

Subtract two numbers to find a **difference**.

Remember,

- 7 + 8 = 15, so 15 − 8 = 7.
- subtracting 9 − 4 is the same as finding the difference of 9 and 4.

Subtract.

	a	b	c	d
1.	15 − 8 = 7	8 − 4 = ____	6 − 1 = ____	7 − 0 = ____
2.	11 − 9 = ____	9 − 0 = ____	13 − 5 = ____	10 − 7 = ____
3.	13 − 4 = ____	15 − 9 = ____	8 − 8 = ____	11 − 6 = ____
4.	3 − 0 = ____	7 − 1 = ____	10 − 5 = ____	4 − 4 = ____
5.	14 − 7 = ____	8 − 2 = ____	16 − 7 = ____	8 − 5 = ____
6.	10 − 2 = ____	4 − 3 = ____	9 − 2 = ____	13 − 6 = ____

Find the differences.

	a	b	c	d	e	f
7.	$\begin{array}{r} 11 \\ -\ 7 \\ \hline 4 \end{array}$	$\begin{array}{r} 9 \\ -3 \\ \hline \end{array}$	$\begin{array}{r} 6 \\ -0 \\ \hline \end{array}$	$\begin{array}{r} 16 \\ -\ 8 \\ \hline \end{array}$	$\begin{array}{r} 10 \\ -\ 9 \\ \hline \end{array}$	$\begin{array}{r} 13 \\ -\ 7 \\ \hline \end{array}$
8.	$\begin{array}{r} 14 \\ -\ 9 \\ \hline \end{array}$	$\begin{array}{r} 13 \\ -\ 3 \\ \hline \end{array}$	$\begin{array}{r} 17 \\ -\ 8 \\ \hline \end{array}$	$\begin{array}{r} 14 \\ -\ 6 \\ \hline \end{array}$	$\begin{array}{r} 9 \\ -5 \\ \hline \end{array}$	$\begin{array}{r} 11 \\ -\ 8 \\ \hline \end{array}$
9.	$\begin{array}{r} 15 \\ -\ 9 \\ \hline \end{array}$	$\begin{array}{r} 8 \\ -1 \\ \hline \end{array}$	$\begin{array}{r} 18 \\ -\ 9 \\ \hline \end{array}$	$\begin{array}{r} 5 \\ -4 \\ \hline \end{array}$	$\begin{array}{r} 5 \\ -0 \\ \hline \end{array}$	$\begin{array}{r} 12 \\ -\ 6 \\ \hline \end{array}$

Subtraction

To subtract, start with the digits in the ones place.

Find: 587 − 234

Subtract the ones.	Subtract the tens.	Subtract the hundreds.
H T O 5 8 **7** − 2 3 **4** 3	H T O 5 **8** 7 − 2 **3** 4 5 3	H T O **5** 8 7 − **2** 3 4 3 5 3

Subtract.

	a	b	c	d	e
1.	T O 2 9 − 6 2 3	T O 7 8 − 8	T O 4 5 − 2	T O 5 9 − 7	T O 3 6 − 5
2.	88 −71	49 −35	70 −30	35 −14	57 −22
3.	779 −344	900 −400	868 − 33	459 −125	987 −753
4.	849 −500	892 −351	764 −610	238 − 15	638 −204

Line up the digits. Then find the differences.

	a	b	c
5.	77 − 42 = ______ 77 −42	954 − 630 = ______	375 − 53 = ______
6.	485 − 60 = ______	753 − 13 = ______	879 − 21 = ______

Regrouping in Subtraction

Start with the digits in the ones place. Regroup as needed.

Find: 630 − 248

630 has no ones. Regroup 3 tens 0 ones as 2 tens 10 ones. Subtract the ones.	Not enough tens. Regroup 6 hundreds 2 tens as 5 hundreds 12 tens. Subtract the tens.	Subtract the hundreds.
H T O 2 10 6 3̸ 0̸ −2 4 8 2	H T O 12 5 2̸ 10 6̸ 3̸ 0̸ −2 4 8 8 2	H T O 12 5 2̸ 10 6̸ 3̸ 0̸ −2 4 8 3 8 2

Subtract.

	a	b	c	d	e
1.	T O 6 13 7̸ 3̸ −3 9 3 4	T O 8 5 −5 9	T O 6 6 −1 8	T O 9 3 −8 5	T O 4 0 −2 7
2.	92 −59	51 −32	70 −47	82 − 5	63 −24
3.	110 − 34	151 − 76	123 − 45	922 −674	530 −280
4.	743 −365	920 −188	818 −492	632 −152	475 −286

Line up the digits. Then find the differences.

	a	b	c
5.	96 − 19 = ______ 96 −19	375 − 89 = ______	863 − 675 = ______

Regrouping Twice in Subtraction

Sometimes you may have to regroup twice before you subtract.

Find: 503 − 234

Not enough ones or tens. Regroup the hundreds.

	H	T	O
	4	10	
	~~5~~	~~0~~	3
−	2	3	4

Regroup the tens.

	H	T	O
		9	
	4	~~10~~	13
	~~5~~	~~0~~	~~3~~
−	2	3	4

Subtract the ones.

	H	T	O
		9	
	4	~~10~~	13
	~~5~~	~~0~~	~~3~~
−	2	3	4
			9

Subtract the tens.

	H	T	O
		9	
	4	~~10~~	13
	~~5~~	~~0~~	~~3~~
−	2	3	4
		6	9

Subtract the hundreds.

	H	T	O
		9	
	4	~~10~~	13
	~~5~~	~~0~~	~~3~~
−	2	3	4
	2	6	9

Subtract.

1.

a

	H	T	O
		10	
	2	~~0~~	18
	~~3~~	~~1~~	~~8~~
−	2	9	9
		1	9

b

	H	T	O
	6	0	4
−	4	5	9

c

	H	T	O
	4	2	5
−	2	3	7

d

	H	T	O
	3	0	3
−		6	4

e

	H	T	O
	2	3	4
−	1	7	8

2. *a* 507 − 149 *b* 804 − 326 *c* 473 − 86 *d* 312 − 235 *e* 901 − 357

3. *a* 600 − 124 *b* 434 − 265 *c* 700 − 570 *d* 831 − 75 *e* 921 − 738

Line up the digits. Then find the differences.

4. *a* 301 − 25 = ______ *b* 423 − 236 = ______ *c* 300 − 142 = ______

  301
− 25

Addition and Subtraction

Sometimes you need to regroup, but sometimes you do not need to regroup.

Find: 612 + 182

No need to regroup.

	H	T	O
	6	1	2
+	1	8	2
	7	9	4

Find: 612 − 182

Not enough tens.
Regroup the hundreds.

	H	T	O
	5	11	
	~~6~~	~~1~~	2
−	1	8	2
	4	3	0

Add. Regroup if needed.

	a	b	c	d	e
1.	$\begin{array}{r} ^{1} \\ 162 \\ +651 \\ \hline 813 \end{array}$	$\begin{array}{r} 276 \\ +198 \\ \hline \end{array}$	$\begin{array}{r} 367 \\ +526 \\ \hline \end{array}$	$\begin{array}{r} 356 \\ +432 \\ \hline \end{array}$	$\begin{array}{r} 157 \\ +259 \\ \hline \end{array}$
2.	$\begin{array}{r} 305 \\ +482 \\ \hline \end{array}$	$\begin{array}{r} 549 \\ +263 \\ \hline \end{array}$	$\begin{array}{r} 461 \\ +307 \\ \hline \end{array}$	$\begin{array}{r} 864 \\ +209 \\ \hline \end{array}$	$\begin{array}{r} 642 \\ +357 \\ \hline \end{array}$

Subtract. Regroup if needed.

	a	b	c	d	e
3.	$\begin{array}{r} 389 \\ -149 \\ \hline 240 \end{array}$	$\begin{array}{r} 403 \\ -152 \\ \hline \end{array}$	$\begin{array}{r} 958 \\ -724 \\ \hline \end{array}$	$\begin{array}{r} 164 \\ -157 \\ \hline \end{array}$	$\begin{array}{r} 843 \\ -621 \\ \hline \end{array}$
4.	$\begin{array}{r} 575 \\ -408 \\ \hline \end{array}$	$\begin{array}{r} 980 \\ -732 \\ \hline \end{array}$	$\begin{array}{r} 497 \\ -134 \\ \hline \end{array}$	$\begin{array}{r} 803 \\ -246 \\ \hline \end{array}$	$\begin{array}{r} 600 \\ -392 \\ \hline \end{array}$

Line up the digits. Then find the sums or differences.

	a	b	c
5.	751 + 324 = ________	675 + 587 = ________	308 − 156 = ________
	$\begin{array}{r} 751 \\ +324 \\ \hline \end{array}$		

Estimation by Rounding Numbers

Rounded numbers tell **approximately** how many. You can use a number line to help you **round** numbers.

Remember, when a number is halfway, always round the number up.

Round 375 to the nearest ten.

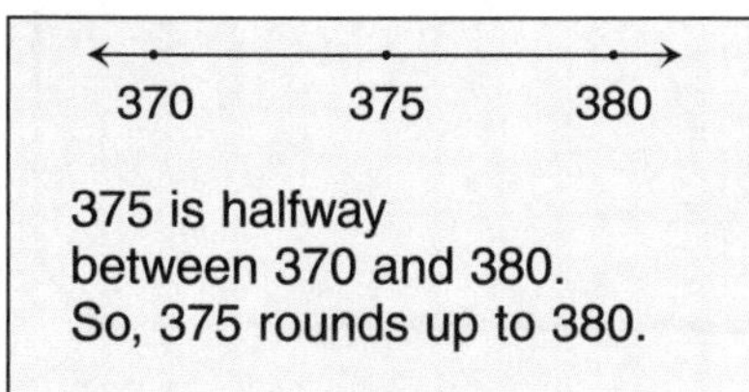

370
375
380
375 is halfway between 370 and 380. So, 375 rounds up to 380.

Round 492 to the nearest hundred.

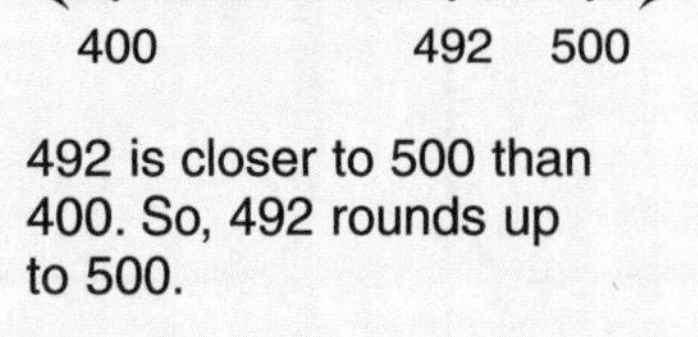

400
492
500
492 is closer to 500 than 400. So, 492 rounds up to 500.

Round 4,120 to the nearest thousand.

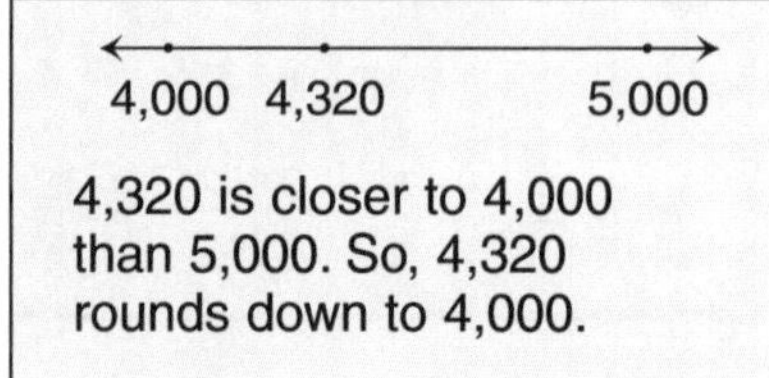

4,000
4,320
5,000
4,320 is closer to 4,000 than 5,000. So, 4,320 rounds down to 4,000.

Round to the nearest ten.

	a	b	c	d
1.	523 *520*	742 ______	258 ______	449 ______
2.	215 ______	869 ______	337 ______	611 ______
3.	876 ______	734 ______	925 ______	862 ______

Round to the nearest hundred.

	a	b	c	d
4.	834 *800*	658 ______	175 ______	717 ______
5.	250 ______	542 ______	326 ______	491 ______
6.	923 ______	789 ______	864 ______	123 ______

Round to the nearest thousand.

	a	b	c	d
7.	1,754 *2,000*	3,958 ______	4,586 ______	9,214 ______
8.	3,621 ______	8,450 ______	6,425 ______	1,642 ______
9.	7,521 ______	1,844 ______	2,453 ______	5,361 ______

Estimation of Sums

To **estimate** a sum, first round each number to the same place value.
Then add the rounded numbers.

Estimate: 64 + 37

Round each number to the same place value. Add.

```
  6 4→  6 0
+ 3 7→+ 4 0
      1 0 0
```

Estimate: 474 + 127

Round each number to the same place value. Add.

```
  4 7 4→  5 0 0
+ 1 2 7→+ 1 0 0
          6 0 0
```

Estimate the sums.

	a	b	c	d
1.	34 → 30 +19 → +20 50	65 → +92 →	49 → +68 →	53 → +21 →
2.	77 → +14 →	29 → +68 →	57 → +23 →	94 → +81 →
3.	635 → +154 →	178 → +482 →	297 → +514 →	782 → +341 →
4.	414 → +308 →	853 → +546 →	671 → +793 →	325 → +230 →

Line up the digits. Then estimate the sums.

	a	b	c
5.	46 + 74 = ________ 46 → 50 +74 → +70	356 + 198 = ________	518 + 732 = ________

Estimation of Differences

To estimate a difference, first round each number to the same place value. Then subtract the rounded numbers.

Remember, when a number is halfway, always round up.

Estimate: 87 − 19

Round each number to the same place value. Subtract.

$$\begin{array}{r} 87 \rightarrow 90 \\ -19 \rightarrow -20 \\ \hline 70 \end{array}$$

Estimate: 387 − 219

Round each number to the same place value. Subtract.

$$\begin{array}{r} 387 \rightarrow 400 \\ -219 \rightarrow -200 \\ \hline 200 \end{array}$$

Estimate the differences.

	a	b	c	d
1.	57 → 60 −38 → −40 20	58 → −46 →	91 → −62 →	83 → −67 →
2.	72 → −64 →	86 → −15 →	53 → − 9 →	96 → −33 →
3.	543 → −264 →	756 → −179 →	435 → −348 →	647 → −253 →
4.	736 → −576 →	352 → −164 →	749 → −185 →	918 → −329 →

Line up the digits. Then estimate the differences.

	a	b	c
5.	92 − 38 = ______ 92 → 90 −38 → −40	872 − 419 = ______	624 − 336 = ______

Problem Solving Method: Identify Extra Information

The tallest building in the United States is the Sears Tower in Chicago, Illinois. It is 1,454 feet tall and has 110 stories. The Empire State Building in New York City has 102 stories. How many more stories does the Sears Tower have than the Empire State Building?

Understand the problem.

- **What do you want to know?**
  how many more stories the Sears Tower has than the Empire State Building

Plan how to solve it.

- **What method can you use?**
  You can identify extra information that is not needed to solve the problem.

Solve it.

- **How can you use this method to solve the problem?**
  Reread the problem. Cross out any unnecessary facts. Then you can focus on the needed facts to solve the problem.

> ~~The tallest building in the United States is the~~ Sears Tower ~~in Chicago, Illinois. It is 1,454 feet tall and~~ has 110 stories. The Empire State Building ~~in New York City~~ has 102 stories. How many more stories does the Sears Tower have than the Empire State Building?

- **What is the answer?**
  110 − 102 = 8
  The Sears Tower has 8 more stories than the Empire State Building.

Look back and check your answer.

- **Is your answer reasonable?**
  You can check subtraction with addition.

$$\begin{array}{r} 110 \\ -102 \\ \hline 8 \end{array} \qquad \begin{array}{r} 102 \\ +\ 8 \\ \hline 110 \end{array}$$

The sum checks.
The answer is reasonable.

In each problem, cross out the extra information. Then solve the problem.

1. Tyrone drove 512 miles on a two-day trip. He went 55 miles per hour. The first day, he drove 305 miles. How many miles did he drive on the second day?

   Answer ______________________

2. Vicky worked 25 hours last week and earned $175. This week she worked 28 hours and earned $196. How much money did she earn altogether?

   Answer ______________________

3. There were 271 events in the 1996 Summer Olympic Games. The United States won 44 gold, 32 silver, and 25 bronze medals. How many medals did the United States win in all?

   Answer ______________________

4. In a vote for favorite ice-cream flavor, chocolate got 659 votes. Vanilla got 781 votes, and 246 people voted for strawberry. How many more people voted for chocolate than for strawberry?

   Answer ______________________

5. One Earth year is about 365 days. One year on Mercury is 88 days. On Mars, a year is 687 days. How much shorter is a year on Mercury than on Earth?

   Answer ______________________

6. A tiger can run 35 miles per hour and sleeps 11 hours a day. A house cat can run 30 miles per hour and sleeps 15 hours a day. How many more hours a day does a house cat sleep than a tiger?

   Answer ______________________

7. Kelly's web site got 129 hits on Friday and 240 hits on Saturday. Tom's web site got 175 hits on Friday and 192 hits on Saturday. How many hits did their sites get altogether on Friday?

   Answer ______________________

UNIT 1 Review

Write the place name for the 7 in each number.

	a	b
1.	36,712 ______	175,689 ______
2.	1,247,953 ______	17,652,810 ______

Write the value of the underlined digit.

	a	b
3.	18,<u>5</u>63 ______	1,<u>3</u>57,942 ______
4.	9<u>4</u>6,358 ______	2,587,4<u>6</u>1 ______

Write each number using digits. Insert commas where needed.

5. nineteen thousand, two hundred six ______

6. four hundred eleven thousand, thirty-five ______

7. two million, six hundred fifty-eight thousand ______

8. seven hundred twenty-three thousand, one hundred four ______

Compare. Write <, >, or =.

	a	b	c
9.	185 ______ 158	37 ______ 37	78 ______ 780
10.	465 ______ 455	1,274 ______ 1,724	3,690 ______ 3,960

Round to the nearest ten.

	a	b	c
11.	452 ______	265 ______	139 ______

Round to the nearest hundred.

	a	b	c
12.	578 ______	364 ______	941 ______

Round to the nearest thousand.

	a	b	c
13.	5,648 ______	4,250 ______	9,461 ______

UNIT 1 Review

Add.

	a	b	c	d	e
14.	541 + 238	416 + 402	174 + 388	518 + 95	943 + 89
15.	395 + 284	199 + 68	752 + 149	354 + 403	865 + 239

Subtract.

	a	b	c	d	e
16.	748 − 26	313 − 108	510 − 346	801 − 528	400 − 317
17.	985 − 254	516 − 238	643 − 99	796 − 284	306 − 298

Estimate the sum or difference.

	a	b	c	d
18.	73→ + 19→	898→ + 356→	84→ − 36→	927→ − 632→
19.	286→ − 89→	453→ + 175→	750→ − 322→	412→ + 645→

Line up the digits. Then add or subtract.

	a	b
20.	47 + 514 + 56 = ________	304 + 819 + 275 = ________
21.	95 − 47 = ________	508 − 372 = ________
22.	736 − 679 = ________	145 + 536 + 75 = ________

Use logic to solve each problem.

23. Three of baseball's top run scorers are Babe Ruth, Ty Cobb, and Willie Mays. Their records are 2,062 runs, 2,245 runs, and 2,174 runs. Mays scored the least. Ruth scored less than Cobb. How many runs did each of the three players score?

Babe Ruth ____________

Ty Cobb ____________

Willie Mays ____________

24. The Mississippi, Yukon, and Missouri are the longest rivers in the United States. Their lengths are 2,315 miles, 1,979 miles, and 2,348 miles. The length of the Yukon does not have 3 hundreds. The Missouri is not the longest. What is the length of each river?

Mississippi River ____________

Yukon River ____________

Missouri River ____________

In each problem, cross out the extra information. Then solve the problem.

25. There are 435 representatives and 100 senators in Congress. Sentors serve 6-year terms and representatives serve 2-year terms. How many members are in Congress altogether?

Answer ____________

26. A person who weighs 100 pounds on Earth would weigh 254 pounds on Jupiter and 38 pounds on Mars. What is the difference between the weight on Earth and the weight on Mars?

Answer ____________

Multiplication Facts Through 5

Multiply two numbers to find a **product**.
Multiplication is a short way to do addition.
4 groups of stars with 3 stars in each group is 12 stars altogether.

We say: **4** times **3** is **12.**

We think: **3 + 3 + 3 + 3 = 12**

We write: **4 × 3 = 12** or

$$\begin{array}{r} 4 \\ \times\ 3 \\ \hline 12 \end{array}$$

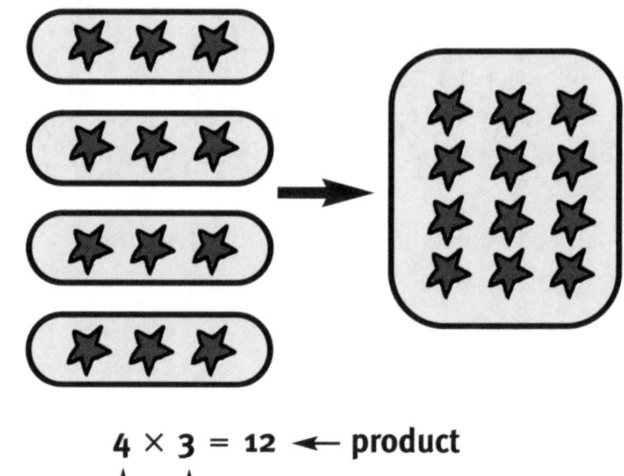

4 × 3 = 12 ← product
↑ ↑
factors

Remember,

- multiplying **4 × 5** is the same as multiplying **5 × 4.**
- multiplying **3 × 2** is the same as finding the product of **3** and **2.**

Multiply.

	a	b	c	d
1.	6 × 4 = 24	7 × 2 = ______	5 × 5 = ______	5 × 3 = ______
2.	3 × 2 = ______	2 × 8 = ______	8 × 3 = ______	0 × 3 = ______
3.	9 × 3 = ______	4 × 4 = ______	1 × 6 = ______	8 × 1 = ______
4.	2 × 2 = ______	2 × 6 = ______	9 × 2 = ______	8 × 5 = ______

Find the products.

	a	b	c	d	e	f
5.	$\begin{array}{r} 6 \\ \times 5 \\ \hline 30 \end{array}$	$\begin{array}{r} 5 \\ \times 3 \\ \hline \end{array}$	$\begin{array}{r} 7 \\ \times 2 \\ \hline \end{array}$	$\begin{array}{r} 2 \\ \times 7 \\ \hline \end{array}$	$\begin{array}{r} 9 \\ \times 1 \\ \hline \end{array}$	$\begin{array}{r} 6 \\ \times 2 \\ \hline \end{array}$
6.	$\begin{array}{r} 7 \\ \times 4 \\ \hline \end{array}$	$\begin{array}{r} 5 \\ \times 8 \\ \hline \end{array}$	$\begin{array}{r} 3 \\ \times 9 \\ \hline \end{array}$	$\begin{array}{r} 4 \\ \times 2 \\ \hline \end{array}$	$\begin{array}{r} 3 \\ \times 3 \\ \hline \end{array}$	$\begin{array}{r} 8 \\ \times 4 \\ \hline \end{array}$
7.	$\begin{array}{r} 1 \\ \times 5 \\ \hline \end{array}$	$\begin{array}{r} 5 \\ \times 4 \\ \hline \end{array}$	$\begin{array}{r} 6 \\ \times 3 \\ \hline \end{array}$	$\begin{array}{r} 8 \\ \times 2 \\ \hline \end{array}$	$\begin{array}{r} 9 \\ \times 5 \\ \hline \end{array}$	$\begin{array}{r} 4 \\ \times 0 \\ \hline \end{array}$

Multiplication Facts for 6 and 7

Find: 6×7

$\begin{array}{r} 6 \\ \times 7 \\ \hline \end{array}$	**Say:** 6 times 7 is 42. **Think:** 7 + 7 + 7 + 7 + 7 + 7 = 42	**Write:**	$\begin{array}{r} 6 \\ \times 7 \\ \hline 42 \end{array}$	or $6 \times 7 = 42$ or $7 \times 6 = 42$

Multiply.

	a	b	c	d	e	f
1.	$\begin{array}{r} 1 \\ \times 6 \\ \hline 6 \end{array}$	$\begin{array}{r} 2 \\ \times 6 \\ \hline \end{array}$	$\begin{array}{r} 3 \\ \times 6 \\ \hline \end{array}$	$\begin{array}{r} 4 \\ \times 6 \\ \hline \end{array}$	$\begin{array}{r} 5 \\ \times 6 \\ \hline \end{array}$	$\begin{array}{r} 6 \\ \times 6 \\ \hline \end{array}$
2.	$\begin{array}{r} 7 \\ \times 6 \\ \hline \end{array}$	$\begin{array}{r} 8 \\ \times 6 \\ \hline \end{array}$	$\begin{array}{r} 9 \\ \times 6 \\ \hline \end{array}$	$\begin{array}{r} 6 \\ \times 5 \\ \hline \end{array}$	$\begin{array}{r} 6 \\ \times 3 \\ \hline \end{array}$	$\begin{array}{r} 6 \\ \times 4 \\ \hline \end{array}$

Find: 7×8

$\begin{array}{r} 7 \\ \times 8 \\ \hline \end{array}$	**Say:** 7 times 8 is 56. **Think:** 8 + 8 + 8+ 8 + 8 + 8 + 8 = 56	**Write:**	$\begin{array}{r} 7 \\ \times 8 \\ \hline 42 \end{array}$	or $7 \times 8 = 56$ or $8 \times 7 = 56$

Find the products.

	a	b	c
3.	$7 \times 5 =$ ______	$7 \times 8 =$ ______	$7 \times 7 =$ ______
4.	$7 \times 4 =$ ______	$7 \times 1 =$ ______	$7 \times 6 =$ ______
5.	$7 \times 0 =$ ______	$7 \times 9 =$ ______	$7 \times 3 =$ ______

Multiplication Facts for 8 and 9

Find: 8×9

$$\begin{array}{r} 9 \\ \times 8 \\ \hline \end{array}$$

Say: 8 times 9 is 72.
Think: 9 + 9 + 9 + 9 + 9 + 9 + 9 + 9 = 72

Write: $\begin{array}{r} 9 \\ \times 8 \\ \hline 72 \end{array}$ or $9 \times 8 = 72$ or $8 \times 9 = 72$

Multiply.

	a	b	c	d	e	f
1.	$3 \times 8 = 24$	4×8	1×8	5×8	6×8	2×8
2.	7×8	9×8	0×8	8×5	8×7	8×4
3.	8×3	8×9	8×6	8×8	8×1	8×2

Find: 9×9

$$\begin{array}{r} 9 \\ \times 9 \\ \hline \end{array}$$

Say: 9 times 9 is 81.
Think: 9 + 9 + 9 + 9 + 9 + 9 + 9 + 9 + 9 = 81

Write: $\begin{array}{r} 9 \\ \times 9 \\ \hline 81 \end{array}$ or $9 \times 9 = 81$

Find the products.

	a	b	c
4.	$9 \times 5 =$ 45	$9 \times 6 =$ ______	$9 \times 4 =$ ______
5.	$9 \times 1 =$ ______	$9 \times 8 =$ ______	$9 \times 0 =$ ______
6.	$9 \times 9 =$ ______	$9 \times 3 =$ ______	$9 \times 7 =$ ______

Multiplication Table

All the basic multiplication facts are given in the table shown.

Use the table to find 3×6.

1. Find 3 in the first factor column.
2. Find 6 in the top factor row.
3. The product is where the column and row meet: $3 \times 6 = 18$

Use the table to find 7×5.

1. Find 7 in the first factor column.
2. Find 5 in the top factor row.
3. The product is where the column and row meet: $7 \times 5 = 35$

×	1	2	3	4	5	6	7	8	9
1	1	2	3	4	5	6	7	8	9
2	2	4	6	8	10	12	14	16	18
3	3	6	9	12	15	18	21	24	27
4	4	8	12	16	20	24	28	32	36
5	5	10	15	20	25	30	35	40	45
6	6	12	18	24	30	36	42	48	54
7	7	14	21	28	35	42	49	56	63
8	8	16	24	32	40	48	56	64	72
9	9	18	27	36	45	54	63	72	81

Multiply. Use the table if needed.

	a	b	c	d	e	f
1.	2×8 = 16	4×3	7×1	6×2	8×9	3×7
2.	4×8	1×8	2×2	9×7	5×8	4×5
3.	5×7	9×6	4×2	6×6	3×2	5×9

Find the products. Use the table if needed.

	a	b	c	d
4.	$5 \times 9 =$ 45	$9 \times 2 =$ ____	$4 \times 7 =$ ____	$4 \times 4 =$ ____
5.	$6 \times 9 =$ ____	$7 \times 6 =$ ____	$8 \times 5 =$ ____	$4 \times 6 =$ ____

Problem-Solving Method: Make a Model

Anita is making a quilt by sewing squares of fabric together. She wants it to have 6 rows with 8 squares in each row. How many fabric squares does she need to make the quilt?

Understand the problem.

- **What do you want to know?**
  how many fabric squares she needs to make the quilt

- **What information is given?**
  The quilt will have 6 rows of 8 squares.

Plan how to solve it.

- **What method can you use?**
  You can make a model of the quilt.

Solve it.

- **How can you use this method to solve the problem?**
  Use tiles to make a model of the quilt.
  Use one tile for each square of the quilt.
  Then count the tiles.

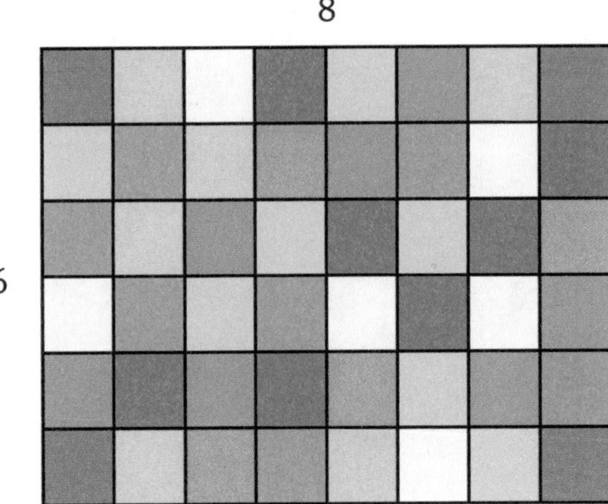

- **What is the answer?**
  Anita needs 48 fabric squares to make the quilt.

Look back and check your answer.

- **Is your answer reasonable?**
  You can check your count with multiplication.

6 rows of 8 squares = 48 squares

6 × 8 = 48

The count and the product are the same.
The answer is reasonable.

Make a model to solve each problem.

1. Kendra put new tiles on her bathroom floor. The floor now has 4 rows with 5 tiles in each row. How many tiles did Kendra use in all?

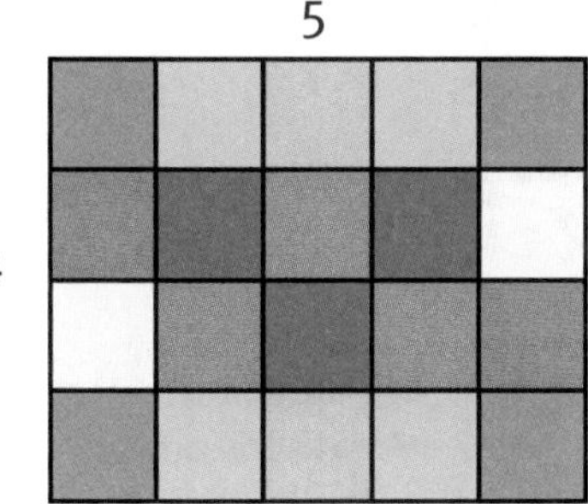

Answer ______________________

2. Tom needs to replace all the panes of glass in a window. The window has 3 rows with 3 panes in each row. How many panes of glass should Tom buy?

Answer ______________________

3. Sue cut a pan of lasagna into 6 rows. Each row has 3 servings of lasagna. How many servings of lasagna did she cut?

Answer ______________________

4. A box of chocolates has 4 rows. Each row has 9 chocolates. How many chocolates are in the box?

Answer ______________________

5. Tony planted 7 rows of tulips with 8 tulips in each row. How many tulips did Tony plant in his garden?

Answer ______________________

Division Facts Through 5

Divide two numbers to find a **quotient**. Division is the opposite of multiplication.

The set of 12 stars is separated into groups of 3 stars each. There are 4 groups.

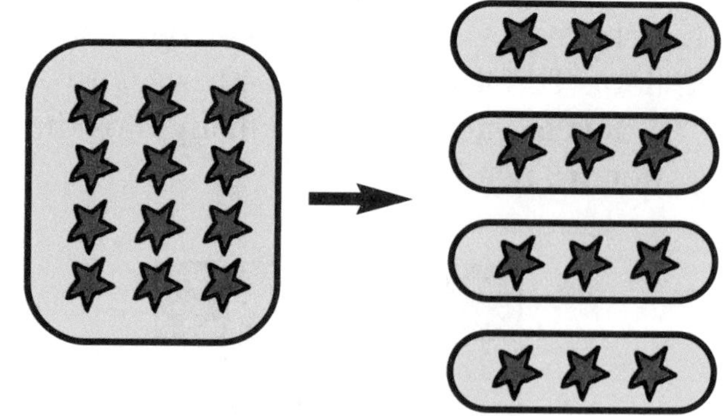

We say: 12 divided by 3 is 4.
We think: 3 × 4 = 12, so 12 ÷ 3 = 4.
We write: 12 ÷ 3 = 4 or $\begin{array}{r}4\\3\overline{)12}\end{array}$

$\begin{array}{r}4\\3\overline{)12}\end{array}$ ← quotient (4), ← dividend (12), ↑ divisor (3)

Remember,
- a number divided by itself is 1.
- 20 ÷ 5 is the same as finding the quotient of 20 divided by 5.

Divide.

	a	b	c	d
1.	32 ÷ 4 = 8	12 ÷ 3 = ____	12 ÷ 4 = ____	15 ÷ 3 = ____
2.	35 ÷ 5 = ____	16 ÷ 2 = ____	27 ÷ 3 = ____	4 ÷ 2 = ____
3.	15 ÷ 5 = ____	3 ÷ 3 = ____	20 ÷ 5 = ____	18 ÷ 2 = ____
4.	20 ÷ 4 = ____	24 ÷ 4 = ____	8 ÷ 4 = ____	28 ÷ 4 = ____
5.	7 ÷ 1 = ____	5 ÷ 5 = ____	21 ÷ 3 = ____	40 ÷ 5 = ____

Find the quotients.

	a	b	c	d	e	f
6.	$\begin{array}{r}6\\5\overline{)30}\end{array}$	$3\overline{)24}$	$4\overline{)16}$	$5\overline{)25}$	$4\overline{)4}$	$2\overline{)14}$
7.	$4\overline{)28}$	$2\overline{)4}$	$1\overline{)3}$	$3\overline{)21}$	$4\overline{)36}$	$2\overline{)8}$
8.	$3\overline{)6}$	$2\overline{)12}$	$5\overline{)45}$	$4\overline{)12}$	$2\overline{)2}$	$5\overline{)10}$

Division Facts for 6 and 7

Find: $42 \div 6$

$6\overline{)42}$ **Say:** 42 divided by 6 is 7.
Think: $6 \times 7 = 42$, so $42 \div 6 = 7$.
Write: $6\overline{)42}$ with quotient 7 or $42 \div 6 = 7$

Divide.

	a	b	c	d	e
1.	$6\overline{)18}$ 3	$6\overline{)36}$	$6\overline{)48}$	$6\overline{)42}$	$6\overline{)6}$
2.	$6\overline{)24}$	$6\overline{)30}$	$6\overline{)12}$	$6\overline{)54}$	$6\overline{)18}$

Find: $42 \div 7$

$7\overline{)42}$ **Say:** 42 divided by 7 is 6.
Think: $7 \times 6 = 42$, so $42 \div 7 = 6$.
Write: $7\overline{)42}$ with quotient 6 or $42 \div 7 = 6$

Find the quotients.

	a	b	c	d
3.	$35 \div 7 =$ 5	$28 \div 7 =$ ____	$56 \div 7 =$ ____	$21 \div 7 =$ ____
4.	$49 \div 7 =$ ____	$7 \div 7 =$ ____	$63 \div 7 =$ ____	$14 \div 7 =$ ____

Write two multiplication sentences and two division sentences for the three numbers given.

	a	b	c
5.	7, 5, and 35	7, 3, and 21	7, 8, and 56
	$7 \times 5 = 35$	____	____
	$5 \times 7 = 35$	____	____
	$35 \div 7 = 5$	____	____
	$35 \div 5 = 7$	____	____

Division Facts for 8 and 9

Find: 64 ÷ 8

8)64 **Say:** 64 divided by 8 is 8.
Think: 8 × 8 = 64, so 64 ÷ 8 = 8.

Write: 8)64 with quotient 8 or 64 ÷ 8 = 8

Divide.

	a	b	c	d	e
1.	8)48 6	8)56	8)72	8)32	8)16
2.	8)8	8)64	8)24	8)40	8)48

Find: 72 ÷ 9

9)72 **Say:** 72 divided by 9 is 8.
Think: 9 × 8 = 72, so 72 ÷ 9 = 8.

Write: 9)72 with quotient 8 or 72 ÷ 9 = 8

Find the quotients.

	a	b	c	d
3.	45 ÷ 9 = 5	18 ÷ 9 = ____	36 ÷ 9 = ____	81 ÷ 9 = ____
4.	63 ÷ 9 = ____	54 ÷ 9 = ____	27 ÷ 9 = ____	9 ÷ 9 = ____

Write two multiplication sentences and two division sentences for the three numbers given.

	a	b	c
5.	5, 9, and 45	6, 9, and 54	3, 9, and 27
	9 × 5 = 45	____	____
	5 × 9 = 45	____	____
	45 ÷ 9 = 5	____	____
	45 ÷ 5 = 9	____	____

Problem-Solving Method: Choose an Operation

A total of 63 people signed up to play in the basketball league. There are 7 teams in the league. All the teams have the same number of players. How many people are on each team?

Understand the problem.

- **What do you want to know?**
  how many people are on each team

- **What information is given?**
  63 people signed up, and there are 7 teams.

Plan how to solve it.

- **What method can you use?**
  You can choose the operation needed to solve it.

Unequal Groups	Equal Groups
Add to combine unequal groups.	**Multiply to combine equal groups.**
Subtract to separate into unequal groups.	**Divide to separate into equal groups.**

Solve it.

- **How can you use this method to solve the problem?**
  Since you need to separate the total into equal groups, you should divide to find how many will be in each group.

$$63 \div 7 = 9$$

63 ↑ total number of players; 7 ↑ number of teams; 9 ↑ number of players on each team

- **What is the answer?**
  There are 9 players on each team.

Look back and check your answer.

- **Is your answer reasonable?**
  You can check division with multiplication.

$63 \div 7 = 9$

Check: $7 \times 9 = 63$

The product matches the dividend.
The answer is reasonable.

Choose an operation to solve each problem. Then solve the problem.

1. Lisa used 48 shells to make 6 necklaces. She used the same number of shells for each necklace. How many shells were on each necklace?

   Operation ____________________

   Answer ____________________

2. The telephone book has 764 pages. There are 316 yellow pages. The rest are white. How many are white pages?

   Operation ____________________

   Answer ____________________

3. Onboard the shuttle *Columbia*, there were 18 mice and 152 rats. How many more rats were onboard than mice?

   Operation ____________________

   Answer ____________________

4. Sara bought a pair of sandals for $32 and a belt for $19. How much did she spend altogether?

   Operation ____________________

   Answer ____________________

5. We brought 5 bags of rolls to the picnic.There were 6 rolls in each bag. How many rolls did we bring?

   Operation ____________________

   Answer ____________________

6. Paul charges $7 per hour for babysitting. How many hours does he have to babysit to earn $28?

   Operation ____________________

   Answer ____________________

Find each answer.

	a		b
1. 4×9	**Say:** ______	$45 \div 5$	**Say:** ______
	Think: ______		**Think:** ______
	Write: ______		**Write:** ______

Multiply.

	a	b	c	d
2.	$1 \times 8 =$ ______	$2 \times 6 =$ ______	$3 \times 3 =$ ______	$4 \times 7 =$ ______
3.	$5 \times 9 =$ ______	$6 \times 4 =$ ______	$7 \times 8 =$ ______	$0 \times 6 =$ ______
4.	$8 \times 4 =$ ______	$9 \times 7 =$ ______	$6 \times 3 =$ ______	$8 \times 5 =$ ______
5.	$4 \times 4 =$ ______	$5 \times 0 =$ ______	$1 \times 7 =$ ______	$6 \times 7 =$ ______

Find the products.

	a	b	c	d	e
6.	1×4	2×3	3×9	4×6	5×4
7.	6×6	7×2	8×8	9×0	7×1
8.	5×3	9×9	0×3	6×5	8×9

Divide.

	a	b	c	d
9.	9 ÷ 1 = ______	14 ÷ 2 = ______	24 ÷ 3 = ______	28 ÷ 4 = ______
10.	45 ÷ 5 = ______	36 ÷ 6 = ______	56 ÷ 7 = ______	64 ÷ 8 = ______
11.	72 ÷ 9 = ______	18 ÷ 2 = ______	12 ÷ 3 = ______	32 ÷ 4 = ______
12.	30 ÷ 5 = ______	54 ÷ 6 = ______	49 ÷ 7 = ______	48 ÷ 8 = ______

Find the quotients.

	a	b	c	d	e
13.	$3\overline{)21}$	$2\overline{)12}$	$5\overline{)20}$	$4\overline{)16}$	$1\overline{)8}$
14.	$6\overline{)42}$	$7\overline{)56}$	$8\overline{)40}$	$9\overline{)81}$	$7\overline{)28}$
15.	$5\overline{)25}$	$4\overline{)16}$	$9\overline{)36}$	$8\overline{)8}$	$6\overline{)24}$
16.	$3\overline{)15}$	$7\overline{)35}$	$9\overline{)54}$	$3\overline{)18}$	$8\overline{)48}$

Write two multiplication sentences and two division sentences for the three numbers given.

	a	b	c
17.	6, 8, and 48	3, 8, and 24	7, 9, and 63
	______	______	______
	______	______	______
	______	______	______
	______	______	______

Make a model to solve each problem.

18. A sheet of postage stamps has 6 rows. Each row has 5 stamps. How many stamps are on 1 sheet?

Answer ______________________

19. A chessboard has 8 rows with 8 squares in each row. How many squares are on a chessboard?

Answer ______________________

Choose an operation to solve each problem. Then solve the problem.

20. Donna set the table for 7 people. She put 3 pieces of silverware at each place at the table. How many pieces of silverware did Donna use in all?

Operation ______________________

Answer ______________________

21. Most glaciers move about 6 feet a day. How many days does it take a glacier to move 30 feet?

Operation ______________________

Answer ______________________

22. In 1998, Randall Cunningham of the Minnesota Vikings completed 259 of his 425 passing attempts. How many of his passes were incomplete?

Operation ______________________

Answer ______________________

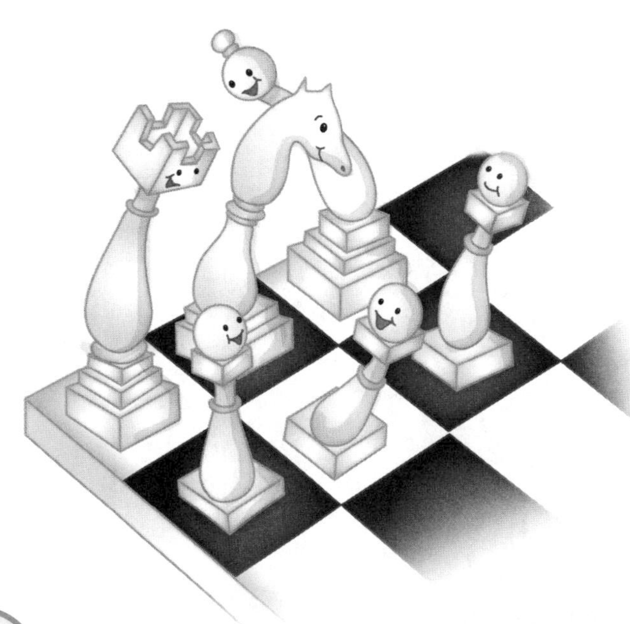

Multiplying by One-digit Numbers to 5

To multiply by a one-digit number, start with the digits in the ones place. Then use your basic multiplication facts.

Remember, zero times any number is zero.

Find: 3 × 20

Multiply the ones. $3 \times 0 = 0$ ones.	Multiply the tens. $3 \times 2 = 60$ tens.
T | O 2 | 0 × | 3 | 0	T | O 2 | 0 × | 3 6 | 0

Find: 4 × 102

Multiply the ones. $4 \times 2 = 8$ ones.	Multiply the tens. $4 \times 0 = 0$ tens.	Multiply the hundreds. $4 \times 1 = 4$ hundreds.
H | T | O 1 | 0 | 2 × | | 4 | | 8	H | T | O 1 | 0 | 2 × | | 4 | 0 | 8	H | T | O 1 | 0 | 2 × | | 4 4 | 0 | 8

Multiply.

	a	b	c	d	e
1.	40 × 2 = 80	30 × 3	10 × 5	20 × 4	60 × 1
2.	11 × 5	22 × 4	32 × 3	54 × 1	43 × 2
3.	130 × 3	210 × 4	140 × 2	290 × 1	330 × 3
4.	342 × 2	311 × 3	243 × 2	100 × 5	202 × 4

Multiply.

	a	b	c	d	e
1.	$\begin{array}{r} 20 \\ \times\ 3 \\ \hline \end{array}$	$\begin{array}{r} 12 \\ \times\ 4 \\ \hline \end{array}$	$\begin{array}{r} 32 \\ \times\ 2 \\ \hline \end{array}$	$\begin{array}{r} 10 \\ \times\ 5 \\ \hline \end{array}$	$\begin{array}{r} 42 \\ \times\ 2 \\ \hline \end{array}$
2.	$\begin{array}{r} 421 \\ \times\ 1 \\ \hline \end{array}$	$\begin{array}{r} 302 \\ \times\ 2 \\ \hline \end{array}$	$\begin{array}{r} 122 \\ \times\ 3 \\ \hline \end{array}$	$\begin{array}{r} 113 \\ \times\ 3 \\ \hline \end{array}$	$\begin{array}{r} 12 \\ \times\ 2 \\ \hline \end{array}$
3.	$\begin{array}{r} 22 \\ \times\ 3 \\ \hline \end{array}$	$\begin{array}{r} 31 \\ \times\ 3 \\ \hline \end{array}$	$\begin{array}{r} 49 \\ \times\ 1 \\ \hline \end{array}$	$\begin{array}{r} 44 \\ \times\ 2 \\ \hline \end{array}$	$\begin{array}{r} 109 \\ \times\ 1 \\ \hline \end{array}$
4.	$\begin{array}{r} 110 \\ \times\ 4 \\ \hline \end{array}$	$\begin{array}{r} 203 \\ \times\ 3 \\ \hline \end{array}$	$\begin{array}{r} 21 \\ \times\ 2 \\ \hline \end{array}$	$\begin{array}{r} 222 \\ \times\ 2 \\ \hline \end{array}$	$\begin{array}{r} 23 \\ \times\ 1 \\ \hline \end{array}$
5.	$\begin{array}{r} 13 \\ \times\ 2 \\ \hline \end{array}$	$\begin{array}{r} 442 \\ \times\ 2 \\ \hline \end{array}$	$\begin{array}{r} 300 \\ \times\ 3 \\ \hline \end{array}$	$\begin{array}{r} 213 \\ \times\ 3 \\ \hline \end{array}$	$\begin{array}{r} 23 \\ \times\ 2 \\ \hline \end{array}$

Line up the digits. Then find the products.

	a	b	c
6.	$99 \times 1 =$ ________ $\begin{array}{r} 99 \\ \times\ 1 \\ \hline \end{array}$	$120 \times 4 =$ ________	$100 \times 2 =$ ________
7.	$41 \times 2 =$ ________	$11 \times 5 =$ ________	$31 \times 3 =$ ________

Multiplying by One-digit Numbers with Regrouping

Multiply the ones first. Regroup when there are ten or more.
Remember, one times any number is that number.

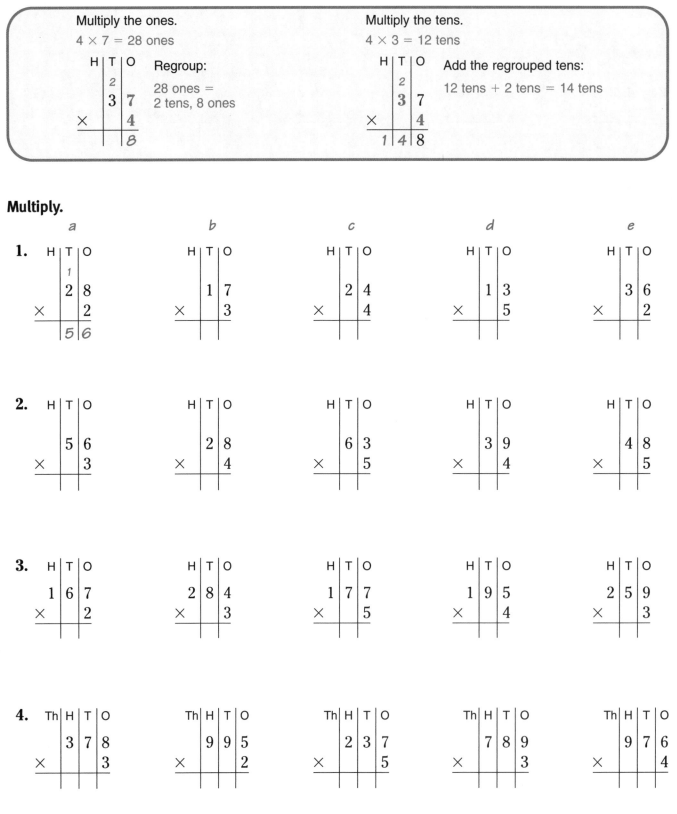

Find: 4×37

Multiply the ones.
$4 \times 7 = 28$ ones

	H	T	O
		2	
		3	7
×			4
			8

Regroup:
28 ones =
2 tens, 8 ones

Multiply the tens.
$4 \times 3 = 12$ tens

	H	T	O
		2	
		3	7
×			4
	1	4	8

Add the regrouped tens:
12 tens + 2 tens = 14 tens

Multiply.

1.

a. 28×2 (regrouped: 1; answer: 56)

b. 17×3

c. 24×4

d. 13×5

e. 36×2

2.

a. 56×3

b. 28×4

c. 63×5

d. 39×4

e. 48×5

3.

a. 167×2

b. 284×3

c. 177×5

d. 195×4

e. 259×3

4.

a. 378×3

b. 995×2

c. 237×5

d. 789×3

e. 976×4

Multiplying Numbers with Zeros by One-digit Numbers

Find: 5 × 206

Multiply the ones. 5 × 6 = 30 ones Regroup.	Multiply the tens. 5 × 0 = 0 tens Add the regrouped tens.	Multiply the hundreds. 5 × 2 = 10 hundreds Regroup.
Th H T O 3 2 0 6 × 5 0	Th H T O 3 2 0 6 × 5 3 0	Th H T O 1 3 2 0 6 × 5 1, 0 3 0

Multiply.

	a	b	c	d
1.	H T O 1 2 0 3 × 4 8 1 2	H T O 1 0 9 × 3	H T O 4 0 3 × 2	H T O 9 0 9 × 1
2.	H T O 1 0 8 × 5	H T O 2 0 7 × 3	H T O 4 0 6 × 2	H T O 2 0 5 × 4
3.	Th H T O 4 0 9 × 3	Th H T O 7 0 6 × 4	Th H T O 8 0 9 × 5	Th H T O 5 0 5 × 2
4.	Th H T O 1, 0 9 2 × 4	Th H T O 1, 0 0 6 × 2	Th H T O 2, 0 4 4 × 3	Th H T O 1, 3 0 0 × 5

Problem-Solving Method: Use Estimation

Giant pandas eat about 35 pounds of bamboo every day. The San Diego Zoo grows its own bamboo crops to feed their 3 pandas. If the zoo can supply 100 pounds of bamboo a day, is it enough to feed the pandas?

Understand the problem.

- **What do you want to know?**
  Is 100 pounds of bamboo enough to feed the pandas each day?

- **What information is given?**
  There are 3 giant pandas in the zoo.
  Each panda eats about 35 pounds of bamboo every day.

Plan how to solve it.

- **What method can you use?**
  Since the problem is not asking for an exact answer, you can use estimation.

Solve it.

- **How can you use this method to solve the problem?**
  Round 35 pounds to 40 pounds and multiply by 3. Remember, it is better to overestimate the amount of food needed than to not have enough.

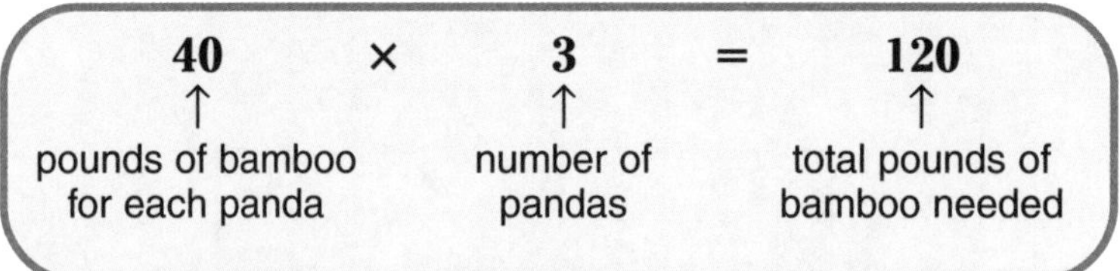

40
×
3
=
120
pounds of bamboo for each panda
number of pandas
total pounds of bamboo needed

- **What is the answer?**
  No, 100 pounds a day is not enough bamboo to feed 3 pandas.

Look back and check your answer.

- **Is your answer reasonable?**
  You can check your estimate by finding the exact answer.

Check:

$$\begin{array}{r} 35 \\ \times\ 3 \\ \hline 105 \end{array} \text{ pounds}$$

The exact answer shows that 100 pounds is not enough. The estimate is reasonable.

Use estimation to solve each problem.

1. On Saturday, 913 people visited the zoo. On Sunday, 789 people visited the zoo. About how many more people visited the zoo on Saturday than on Sunday?

Answer ______________________

2. The Ironman triathlon is a three-part race. First, racers swim about 2 miles. Then they bike 112 miles. Finally, they run 26 miles. About how many miles long is the whole race?

Answer ______________________

3. The world's fastest fish is the sailfish. It can swim 68 miles per hour. About how many miles can a sailfish swim in 3 hours?

Answer ______________________

4. Super Video sold 385 movies this week. If they sell that much every week, about how many movies will they sell in 4 weeks?

Answer ______________________

5. Sara charges $29 to mow one lawn. About how much will she earn if she mows 4 lawns?

Answer ______________________

Multiplying by 6 and 7

Find: 6 × 324

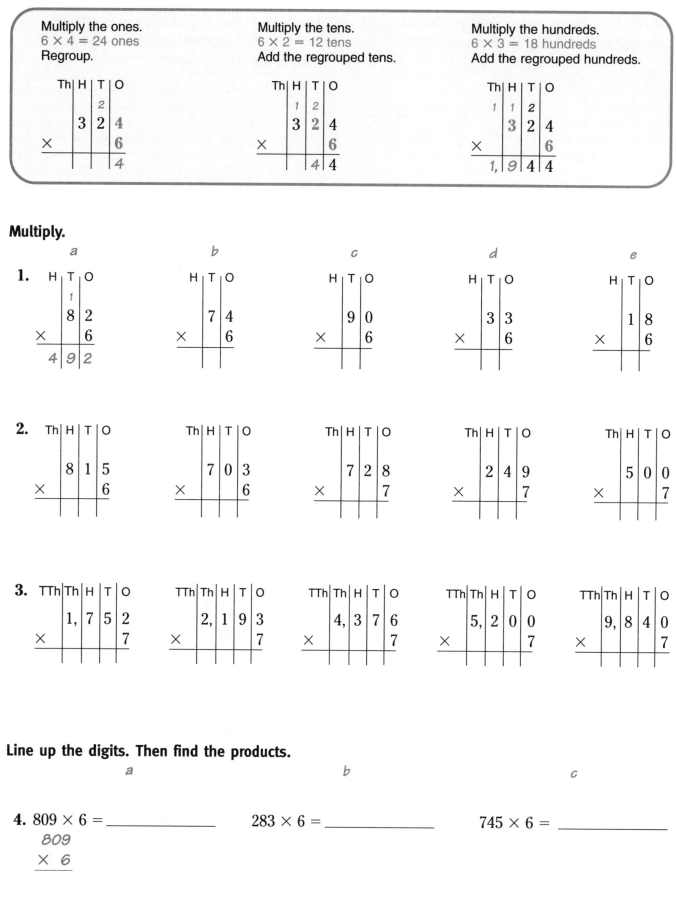

Multiply the ones.
6 × 4 = 24 ones
Regroup.

Th	H	T	O
		2	
	3	2	4
×			6
			4

Multiply the tens.
6 × 2 = 12 tens
Add the regrouped tens.

Th	H	T	O
	1	2	
	3	2	4
×			6
		4	4

Multiply the hundreds.
6 × 3 = 18 hundreds
Add the regrouped hundreds.

Th	H	T	O
1	1	2	
	3	2	4
×			6
1,	9	4	4

Multiply.

1.

a

H	T	O
	1	
	8	2
×		6
4	9	2

b

H	T	O
	7	4
×		6

c

H	T	O
	9	0
×		6

d

H	T	O
	3	3
×		6

e

H	T	O
	1	8
×		6

2.

a

Th	H	T	O
	8	1	5
×			6

b

Th	H	T	O
	7	0	3
×			6

c

Th	H	T	O
	7	2	8
×			7

d

Th	H	T	O
	2	4	9
×			7

e

Th	H	T	O
	5	0	0
×			7

3.

a

TTh	Th	H	T	O
	1,	7	5	2
×				7

b

TTh	Th	H	T	O
	2,	1	9	3
×				7

c

TTh	Th	H	T	O
	4,	3	7	6
×				7

d

TTh	Th	H	T	O
	5,	2	0	0
×				7

e

TTh	Th	H	T	O
	9,	8	4	0
×				7

Line up the digits. Then find the products.

a

4. 809 × 6 = ______________

809
× 6

b

283 × 6 = ______________

c

745 × 6 = ______________

Multiplying by 8 and 9

Find: 8 × 419

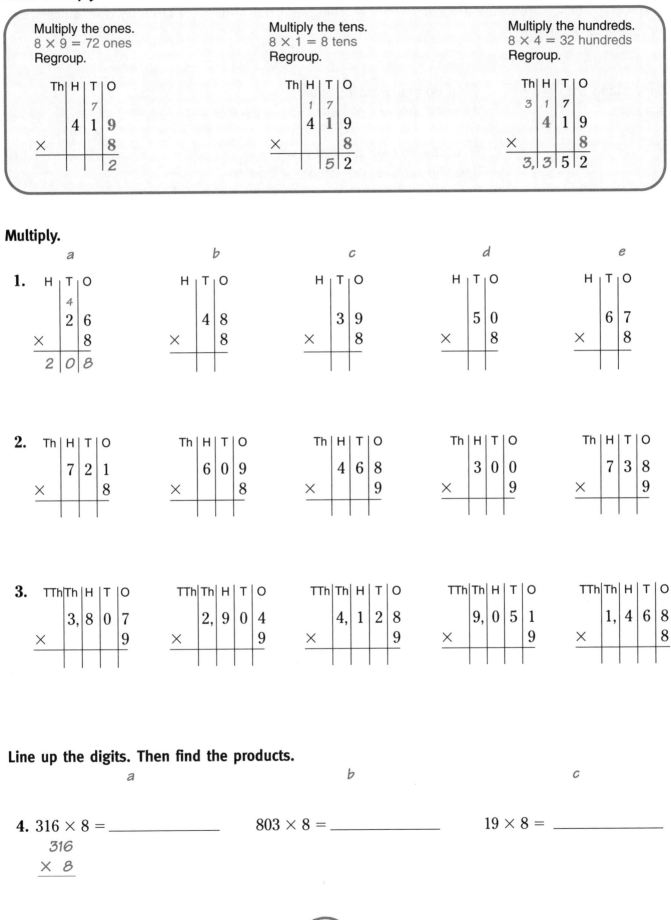

Multiply the ones. $8 \times 9 = 72$ ones Regroup.	Multiply the tens. $8 \times 1 = 8$ tens Regroup.	Multiply the hundreds. $8 \times 4 = 32$ hundreds Regroup.
Th H T O: (7) 4 1 9 × 8 = 2	Th H T O: (1)(7) 4 1 9 × 8 = 5 2	Th H T O: (3)(1)(7) 4 1 9 × 8 = 3,3 5 2

Multiply.

	a	b	c	d	e
1.	(4) 26 × 8 = 208	48 × 8	39 × 8	50 × 8	67 × 8
2.	721 × 8	609 × 8	468 × 9	300 × 9	738 × 9
3.	3,807 × 9	2,904 × 9	4,128 × 9	9,051 × 9	1,468 × 8

Line up the digits. Then find the products.

	a	b	c
4.	$316 \times 8 =$ ______ (316 × 8)	$803 \times 8 =$ ______	$19 \times 8 =$ ______

Problem-Solving Method: Solve Multi-Step Problems

An average shower uses 37 gallons of water. One washing machine load uses 50 gallons of water. In the last week, Karen took a shower every morning and did 3 loads of laundry. How much water did she use altogether?

Understand the problem.

- **What do you want to know?**
  the total amount of water Karen used

- **What information do you know?**
  One shower uses 37 gallons of water.
  One washing machine load uses 50 gallons of water.
  Karen took 7 showers and did 3 loads of wash.

Plan how to solve it.

- **What method can you use?**
  You can separate the problem into steps.

Solve it.

- **How can you use this method to solve the problem?**
  First find how much water each activity used.
  Then add those amounts to find the total.

Step 1 Showers	Step 2 Laundry	Step 3 Total
37 ← gallons per shower	50 ← gallons per load	259 ← shower total
× 7 ← number of showers	× 3 ← number of loads	+150 ← laundry total
259 gallons	150 gallons	409 gallons

- **What is the answer?**
  Karen used a total of 409 gallons of water.

Look back and check your answer.

- **Is your answer reasonable?**
  You can add to check your multiplication.

  37 + 37 + 37 + 37 + 37 + 37 + 37 + 50 + 50 + 50 = 409

  The answer matches the sum.
  The answer is reasonable.

Separate each problem into steps to solve.

1. Angelo had $100. He bought 6 CDs for $13 each. How much money did he have left?

Answer ______________________

2. One gram of fat has 9 calories. One egg has 6 grams of fat. How many calories are in 4 eggs?

Answer ______________________

3. On average, a dragonfly flies 18 miles per hour. A bumblebee flies 11 miles per hour. If both insects fly for 6 hours, how much farther will the dragonfly go?

Answer ______________________

4. Brenda planted 9 rows of daisies and 8 rows of tulips. She fit 18 flowers in each row. How many flowers did she plant altogether?

Answer ______________________

5. The average chimpanzee weighs 110 pounds. An orangutan weighs about 55 pounds more than a chimpanzee. A gorilla can weigh 3 times as much as a orangutan. How much does an average gorilla weigh?

Answer ______________________

Multiply.

	a	b	c	d	e
1.	12×4	21×3	30×5	404×2	432×1
2.	75×6	42×9	103×7	200×8	452×7
3.	342×3	125×4	160×4	306×5	548×3
4.	$2,594 \times 6$	$4,320 \times 8$	954×7	$3,015 \times 9$	$2,857 \times 8$

Line up the digits. Then find the products.

	a	b	c
5.	$20 \times 5 =$ ______	$94 \times 3 =$ ______	$36 \times 8 =$ ______
6.	$83 \times 2 =$ ______	$45 \times 8 =$ ______	$104 \times 6 =$ ______
7.	$257 \times 7 =$ ______	$1,950 \times 2 =$ ______	$2,901 \times 4 =$ ______

Use estimation to solve each problem.

8. Leroy has $200 to buy food for the party. If each pizza costs $16, does he have enough money to buy 9 pizzas?

Answer ______________________

9. The Concord jet cruises at 1,450 miles per hour. About how many miles can it fly in 3 hours?

Answer ______________________

10. Kendra ordered 500 T-shirts. She needs to deliver 125 T-shirts to each of her 7 stores. Did she order enough?

Answer ______________________

Separate each problem into steps to solve.

11. The theater seats 176 people. There are 3 shows on Saturday and 2 shows on Sunday. How many more people can see the show on Saturday than on Sunday?

Answer ______________________

12. Brian has two jobs. He works 20 hours a week at a radio station, where he makes $9 an hour. He also earns $75 a week walking dogs. How much does he make each week altogether?

Answer ______________________

unit 4

Dividing by One-Digit Numbers

Dividing Two-digit Numbers by 2, 3, 4, and 5

To divide by a one-digit **divisor**, start with the largest place value of the **dividend**. Then use your division facts. Multiply and subtract.

Remember, you can check your division by multiplying.

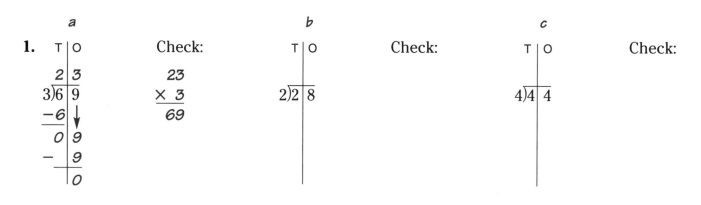

Find: 68 ÷ 2

Divide.

```
 T|O
2)6|8
```

Multiply and subtract.

```
 T|O
  3|
2)6|8
 -6|↓
  0|8
```

6 ÷ 2 = 3
Put a 3 in the tens place. Multiply and subtract. Bring down the 8 ones.

$2\overline{)6}$ = 3

Multiply and subtract.

```
 T|O
  3|4
2)6|8
 -6|↓
  0|8
 - |8
   |0
```

8 ÷ 2 = 4
Put a 4 in the ones place. Multiply and subtract.

$2\overline{)8}$ = 4

Check:
Multiply divisor and quotient.

```
 34
× 2
 68
```

Divide. Check.

1. a

```
 T|O
  2|3
3)6|9
 -6|↓
  0|9
 - |9
   |0
```

Check:

```
 23
× 3
 69
```

b

```
 T|O
2)2|8
```

Check:

c

```
 T|O
4)4|4
```

Check:

Set up the problems. Then find the quotients.

	a	b	c
2.	242 ÷ 2 = ________	84 ÷ 2 = ________	399 ÷ 3 = ________

$2\overline{)242}$

Dividing Three-digit Numbers by 2, 3, 4, and 5

To divide, first choose a **trial quotient**. Start with the largest place value in the dividend. Then multiply and subtract.

Find: 208 ÷ 4

Divide.

H	T	O
4)2	0	8

$2 < 4$
4 does not go into 2.

Move to the next place value.

Multiply and subtract.

H	T	O
	5	
4)2	**0**	8
−2	0	↓
	0	8

$4\overline{)20}$ = 5

Multiply and subtract.

H	T	O
	5	2
4)2	0	**8**
−2	0	
	0	**8**
	−	8
		0

$4\overline{)8}$ = 2

Check:

Multiply divisor and quotient.

$$\begin{array}{r} 52 \\ \times\ 4 \\ \hline 208 \end{array}$$

Divide. Check.

1.

a

H	T	O
	7	1
4)2	8	4
−2	8	↓
	0	4
−		4
		0

Check:

$$\begin{array}{r} 71 \\ \times\ 4 \\ \hline 284 \end{array}$$

b

H	T	O
2)1	0	8

Check:

c

H	T	O
5)2	0	5

Check:

Set up the problems. Then find the quotients.

	a	*b*	*c*
2.	255 ÷ 5 = ________	120 ÷ 4 = ________	129 ÷ 3 = ________
	$5\overline{)255}$		
3.	155 ÷ 5 = ________	104 ÷ 2 = ________	216 ÷ 3 = ________

Dividing with Remainders

Sometimes a number cannot be divided into even groups. Then there is a **remainder**, or an amount left over.

Find: 26 ÷ 5

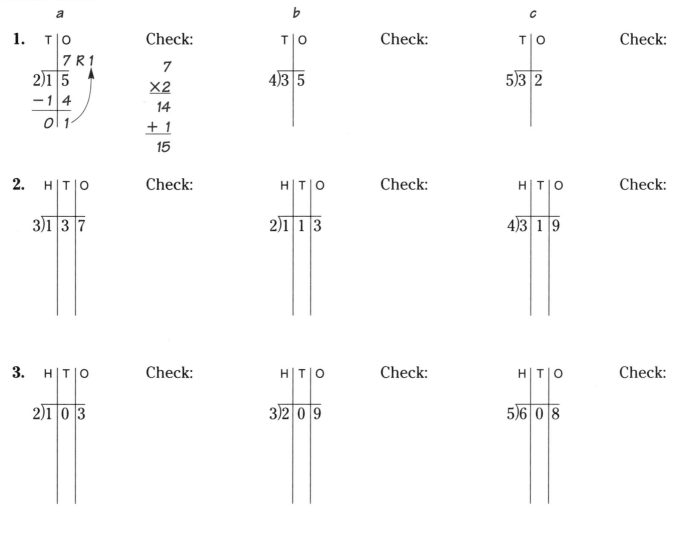

Divide.	Multiply and subtract.	Write the remainder in the quotient.	Check: Multiply divisor and quotient. Add the remainder.
$5\overline{)26}$	$5\overline{)26}$ quotient 5; -25; 01	$5\overline{)26}$ quotient 5 R1; -25; 01	$5 \times 5 = 25$; $25 + 1 = 26$
$2 < 5$ 5 does not go into 2.	$5\overline{)26}$ is 5 with a remainder of 1.		

Divide. Check.

	a		b		c	
1.	$2\overline{)15}$ = 7 R1; -14; 01	Check: $7 \times 2 = 14$; $14 + 1 = 15$	$4\overline{)35}$	Check:	$5\overline{)32}$	Check:
2.	$3\overline{)137}$	Check:	$2\overline{)113}$	Check:	$4\overline{)319}$	Check:
3.	$2\overline{)103}$	Check:	$3\overline{)209}$	Check:	$5\overline{)608}$	Check:

Divide. Check.

	a	*b*	*c*
1.	$4\overline{)25}$	$5\overline{)47}$	$3\overline{)261}$
2.	$3\overline{)245}$	$5\overline{)100}$	$7\overline{)52}$
3.	$4\overline{)206}$	$3\overline{)22}$	$2\overline{)111}$
4.	$3\overline{)109}$	$2\overline{)13}$	$4\overline{)104}$

Set up the problems. Then find the quotients.

	a	*b*	*c*
5.	$218 \div 5 =$ __________	$33 \div 4 =$ __________	$201 \div 3 =$ __________
	$5\overline{)218}$		
6.	$19 \div 2 =$ __________	$118 \div 3 =$ __________	$304 \div 5 =$ __________

Problem-Solving Method: Use Guess and Check

Anthony's band won $35 in a song contest. When they divided the prize money evenly, they had $2 left over. Each band member got more than $10. How many people are in the band?

Understand the problem.

- **What do you want to know?**
  the number of people in the band

- **What information is given?**
  Clue 1: When they divided $35 evenly, they had $2 left over.
  Clue 2: Each band member got more than $10.

Plan how to solve it.

- **What method can you use?**
  Since there is no clear way to solve the problem, you can guess first and then check your answer.

Solve it.

- **How can you use this method to solve the problem?**
  Guess the number of people in the band. Then divide $35 by your guess to check. Keep guessing and checking until you find a remainder of $2 and a quotient greater than $10.

Guess	5 band members	4 band members	3 band members
Check	$\begin{array}{r} 7 \\ 5\overline{)35} \\ -35 \\ \hline 0 \end{array}$ No remainder Does not check. Keep guessing.	$\begin{array}{r} 8 \\ 4\overline{)35} \\ -32 \\ \hline 3 \end{array}$ Remainder 3 Does not check. Keep guessing.	$\begin{array}{r} 11 \text{ R } 2 \\ 3\overline{)35} \\ -3 \\ \hline 05 \\ -3 \\ \hline 2 \end{array}$ Remainder 2, and 11 > 10

- **What is the answer?**
  There are 3 people in the band.

Look back and check your answer.

- **Is your answer reasonable?**
  You can check division with multiplication.

$$\begin{array}{r} 11 \leftarrow \text{money each received} \\ \times\ 3 \leftarrow \text{people in band} \\ \hline 33 \\ +\ 2 \leftarrow \text{money left over} \\ \hline 35 \leftarrow \text{total prize money} \end{array}$$

The multiplication checks and the guess satisfies both clues.
The answer is reasonable.

Guess and check to solve each problem.

1. Will had 47 photographs to put in his album. When he divided them evenly onto 11 pages, he had 3 left over. How many photographs did Will put on each page?

Answer ______________________

2. Stacey has 4 United States coins. Their total value is 31 cents. What coins does Stacey have? How many of each coin?

Answer ______________________

3. Jenna is 5 years older than Darius. The sum of their ages is 21 years. How old are Jenna and Darius?

Answer ______________________

4. The warehouse packed the same number of shirts in 4 boxes. After packing a shipment of 17 shirts, they had 1 left over. How many shirts did they pack in each box?

Answer ______________________

5. Tickets to the fair cost twice as much for an adult as for a child. Mr. Chin spent $9 on tickets for himself and his son. What is the price of each ticket?

Answer ______________________

Dividing by 6 and 7

Find: 256 ÷ 6

Divide.

$6\overline{)256}$

2 < 6

6 does not go into 2.

Multiply and subtract.

$$\begin{array}{r} 4 \\ 6\overline{)256} \\ -24\downarrow \\ \hline 16 \end{array}$$

$6\overline{)25}$ is about 4.

Multiply and subtract.

$$\begin{array}{r} 42\text{ R }4 \\ 6\overline{)256} \\ -24 \\ \hline 16 \\ -12 \\ \hline 4 \end{array}$$

$6\overline{)16}$ is about 2.

Check:

Multiply divisor and quotient.

Add the remainder.

$$\begin{array}{r} 42 \\ \times\ 6 \\ \hline 252 \\ +\ 4 \\ \hline 256 \end{array}$$

Divide. Check.

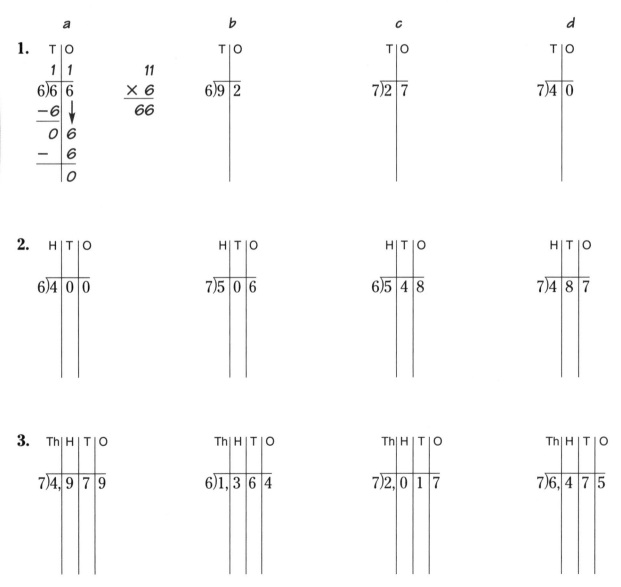

	a	b	c	d
1.	$\begin{array}{r} 11 \\ 6\overline{)66} \\ -6\downarrow \\ \hline 06 \\ -\ 6 \\ \hline 0 \end{array}$ $\begin{array}{r} 11 \\ \times 6 \\ \hline 66 \end{array}$	$6\overline{)92}$	$7\overline{)27}$	$7\overline{)40}$
2.	$6\overline{)400}$	$7\overline{)506}$	$6\overline{)548}$	$7\overline{)487}$
3.	$7\overline{)4,979}$	$6\overline{)1,364}$	$7\overline{)2,017}$	$7\overline{)6,475}$

Dividing by 8 and 9

Divide. Check.

	a	b	c	d
1.	$8\overline{)39}$	$8\overline{)97}$	$9\overline{)52}$	$9\overline{)20}$
2.	$8\overline{)898}$	$9\overline{)700}$	$8\overline{)408}$	$9\overline{)243}$
3.	$8\overline{)3,288}$	$8\overline{)1,111}$	$9\overline{)1,899}$	$9\overline{)8,901}$

Set up the problems. Then find the quotients.

	a	b	c
4.	$97 \div 8 =$ __________ $8\overline{)97}$	$263 \div 9 =$ __________	$7,707 \div 8 =$ __________
5.	$8,401 \div 9 =$ __________	$496 \div 8 =$ __________	$557 \div 9 =$ __________

Problem-Solving Method: Write a Number Sentence

The moon's gravity is one-sixth that of Earth's. This means that an object's Earth weight divided by 6 is its moon weight. If an astronaut weighs 192 pounds on Earth, how much will he weigh on the moon?

Understand the problem.

- **What do you want to know?**
  the astronaut's weight on the moon

- **What information is given?**
  Weight on the moon is the weight on Earth divided by 6.
  The astronaut weighs 192 pounds on Earth.

Plan how to solve it.

- **What method can you use?**
  You can write a number sentence to model the problem.

Solve it.

- **How can you use this method to solve the problem?**
  Since you know his weight on the moon is his Earth weight divided by 6, you can write a division number sentence.

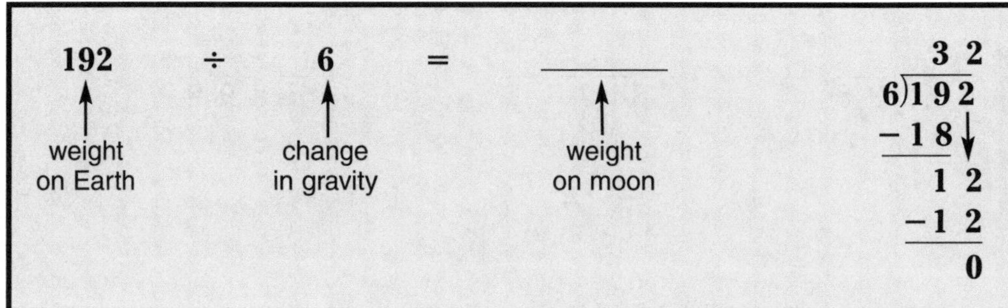

- **What is the answer?**
  The astronaut will weigh 32 pounds on the moon.

Look back and check your answer.

- **Is your answer reasonable?**

You can check division with multiplication.

$$\begin{array}{r} 32 \\ \times\ 6 \\ \hline 192 \end{array}$$

32 ← weight on Moon
× 6 ← change in gravity
192 ← weight on Earth

The product matches the dividend.
The answer is reasonable.

Write a number sentence to solve each problem.

1. Between 1969 and 1972, the *Apollo* missions brought back about 840 pounds of lunar rock samples. How much did the rocks weigh on the moon? (Earth weight ÷ 6 = moon weight)

Answer ______________________

2. The Brooklyn Bridge in New York is 6,016 feet long. The Golden Gate Bridge in San Francisco is 1,816 feet shorter. How long is the Golden Gate Bridge?

Answer ______________________

3. Every year, Joel gives the same amount of money to charity. In the past 8 years he has given a total of $1,400. How much money does he give each year?

Answer ______________________

4. In 1996, Shannon Lucid spent 189 days in space. That is longer than any other female astronaut. How many weeks was she in space?

Answer ______________________

5. At 8 inches long, the pygmy is the smallest shark in the world. The largest is the whale shark. It can be 75 times as long as a pygmy shark. How long is an average whale shark?

Answer ______________________

6. The 3,420 new library books are to be shared equally by 9 libraries. How many books will each library get?

Answer ______________________

UNIT 4 Review

Divide. Check.

	a	b	c	d
1.	$3\overline{)36}$	$4\overline{)84}$	$6\overline{)79}$	$7\overline{)85}$
2.	$8\overline{)376}$	$9\overline{)423}$	$2\overline{)116}$	$5\overline{)205}$
3.	$3\overline{)78}$	$5\overline{)75}$	$6\overline{)329}$	$7\overline{)250}$
4.	$8\overline{)69}$	$9\overline{)53}$	$2\overline{)273}$	$3\overline{)194}$

Set up the problems. Then find the quotients.

	a	b	c
5.	96 ÷ 3 = ____________	101 ÷ 7 = ____________	43 ÷ 4 = ____________
6.	680 ÷ 5 = ____________	1,339 ÷ 9 = ____________	5,107 ÷ 6 = ____________

Guess and check to solve each problem.

7. Anna had 84 books to place on 9 shelves. She put the same number of books on each shelf. There were 3 books left over. How many books did she put on each shelf?

Answer ______________________________

8. Ryan used 50 apples to make several pies. He put the same number of apples in each pie. He had 1 apple left over. How many pies did he make?

Answer ______________________________

Write a number sentence to solve each problem.

9. Jamal delivers the same number of newspapers every morning. In one week, he delivers 203 newspapers. How many does he deliver each morning?

Answer ______________________________

10. In 8 hours of work, Tyler earns $136. How much does he make each hour?

Answer ______________________________

11. The aquarium has 275 angelfish. The same number of angelfish live in each of the aquarium's 5 tanks. How many angelfish are in each tank?

Answer ______________________________

Unit 5
Multiplying and Dividing Larger Numbers

Multiplying by Tens and Hundreds

To multiply tens, multiply the non-zero numbers. Then write one zero. To multiply hundreds, multiply the non-zero numbers. Then write two zeros.

Find: 30 × 4

Long Way Multiply by 4 ones.	*Short Way* Multiply the non-zero numbers. Write one zero for tens in the product.
$\begin{array}{r} 4 \rightarrow \\ \times\ 30 \rightarrow \\ \hline 120 \end{array}$	$\begin{array}{l} \ \ 4 \\ \times 3 \text{ tens} \\ \hline 12 \text{ tens} = 120 \end{array}$

Find: 3 × 500

Long Way Multiply by 3 ones.	*Short Way* Multiply the non-zero numbers. Write two zeros for hundreds in the product.
$\begin{array}{r} 500 \rightarrow \\ \times\ 3 \rightarrow \\ \hline 1,500 \end{array}$	$\begin{array}{l} \ \ 5 \text{ hundreds} \\ \times 3 \\ \hline 15 \text{ hundreds} = 1,500 \end{array}$

Multiply. Use the short way.

	a	b
1.	$\begin{array}{rl} 10 \rightarrow & \underline{\ 1\ } \text{ ten} \\ \times\ 6 \rightarrow & \times\ 6 \\ & 6 \text{ tens} = 60 \end{array}$	$\begin{array}{rl} 40 \rightarrow & \underline{\quad} \text{ tens} \\ \times\ 8 \rightarrow & \times \underline{\quad} \\ & \text{tens} = \end{array}$
2.	$\begin{array}{rl} 3 \rightarrow & \underline{\quad} \\ \times 80 \rightarrow & \times \underline{\quad} \text{ tens} \\ & \text{tens} = \end{array}$	$\begin{array}{rl} 9 \rightarrow & \underline{\quad} \\ \times 10 \rightarrow & \times \underline{\quad} \text{ tens} \\ & \text{tens} = \end{array}$
3.	$\begin{array}{rl} 100 \rightarrow & \underline{\quad} \text{ hundred} \\ \times\ 4 \rightarrow & \times \underline{\quad} \\ & \text{hundreds} = \end{array}$	$\begin{array}{rl} 800 \rightarrow & \underline{\quad} \text{ hundreds} \\ \times\ 2 \rightarrow & \times \underline{\quad} \\ & \text{hundreds} = \end{array}$
4.	$\begin{array}{rl} 7 \rightarrow & \underline{\quad} \\ \times 200 \rightarrow & \times \underline{\quad} \text{ hundreds} \\ & \text{hundreds} = \end{array}$	$\begin{array}{rl} 6 \rightarrow & \underline{\quad} \\ \times 300 \rightarrow & \times \underline{\quad} \text{ hundreds} \\ & \text{hundreds} = \end{array}$

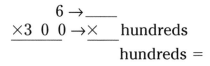

Multiply. Use the short way.

	a	b	c	d	e
1.	30×3	50×9	70×5	80×4	90×7
2.	9×60	7×30	9×80	3×60	5×50
3.	600×6	700×8	200×6	300×9	800×4
4.	5×700	7×600	8×800	6×400	3×600

Multiply. Use the short way.

	a	b	c
5.	$10 \times 5 =$ ______	$20 \times 3 =$ ______	$10 \times 7 =$ ______
6.	$50 \times 2 =$ ______	$40 \times 6 =$ ______	$70 \times 3 =$ ______
7.	$5 \times 90 =$ ______	$7 \times 50 =$ ______	$8 \times 90 =$ ______
8.	$40 \times 9 =$ ______	$70 \times 7 =$ ______	$80 \times 6 =$ ______
9.	$5 \times 300 =$ ______	$8 \times 600 =$ ______	$9 \times 700 =$ ______
10.	$900 \times 9 =$ ______	$800 \times 9 =$ ______	$500 \times 8 =$ ______

Multiplying Two-digit Numbers by Two-digit Numbers

To multiply two-digit numbers, multiply by the ones first. Then multiply by the tens. Then add these two **partial products**.

Find: 25 × 13

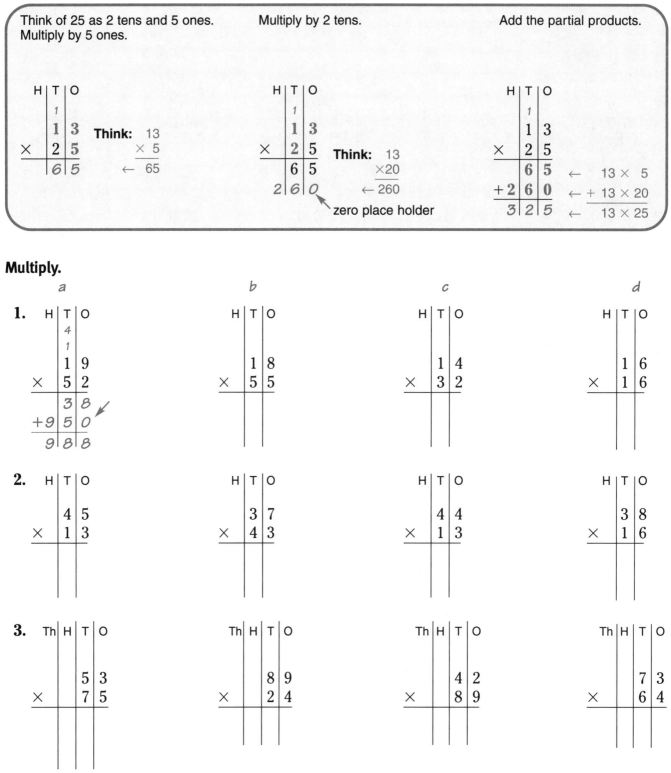

Think of 25 as 2 tens and 5 ones. Multiply by 5 ones.

H	T	O
	1	
	1	3
×	2	5
	6	5

Think: 13 × 5 → 65

Multiply by 2 tens.

H	T	O
	1	
	1	3
×	2	5
	6	5
2	6	0

Think: 13 × 20 → 260

zero place holder

Add the partial products.

H	T	O	
	1		
	1	3	
×	2	5	
	6	5	← 13 × 5
+2	6	0	← + 13 × 20
3	2	5	← 13 × 25

Multiply.

1. a. 19×52 (worked: 4, 1 carried; 38; +950; 988) b. 18×55 c. 14×32 d. 16×16

2. a. 45×13 b. 37×43 c. 44×13 d. 38×16

3. a. 53×75 b. 89×24 c. 42×89 d. 73×64

Multiply.

	a	b	c	d	e
1.	$\begin{array}{r} 28 \\ \times 33 \\ \hline \end{array}$	$\begin{array}{r} 62 \\ \times 71 \\ \hline \end{array}$	$\begin{array}{r} 22 \\ \times 58 \\ \hline \end{array}$	$\begin{array}{r} 49 \\ \times 16 \\ \hline \end{array}$	$\begin{array}{r} 84 \\ \times 59 \\ \hline \end{array}$
2.	$\begin{array}{r} 23 \\ \times 92 \\ \hline \end{array}$	$\begin{array}{r} 18 \\ \times 66 \\ \hline \end{array}$	$\begin{array}{r} 42 \\ \times 12 \\ \hline \end{array}$	$\begin{array}{r} 34 \\ \times 24 \\ \hline \end{array}$	$\begin{array}{r} 81 \\ \times 37 \\ \hline \end{array}$
3.	$\begin{array}{r} 44 \\ \times 29 \\ \hline \end{array}$	$\begin{array}{r} 32 \\ \times 17 \\ \hline \end{array}$	$\begin{array}{r} 94 \\ \times 35 \\ \hline \end{array}$	$\begin{array}{r} 65 \\ \times 19 \\ \hline \end{array}$	$\begin{array}{r} 47 \\ \times 25 \\ \hline \end{array}$

Line up the digits. Then find the products.

	a	b	c
4.	$54 \times 46 =$ ________ $\begin{array}{r} 54 \\ \times 46 \\ \hline \end{array}$	$55 \times 21 =$ ________	$15 \times 39 =$ ________
5.	$36 \times 31 =$ ________	$83 \times 52 =$ ________	$85 \times 11 =$ ________

Multiplying Three-digit Numbers by Two-digit Numbers

To multiply three-digit numbers by two-digit numbers, multiply by the ones first. Then multiply by the tens. Then add these two partial products.

Find: 64 × 753

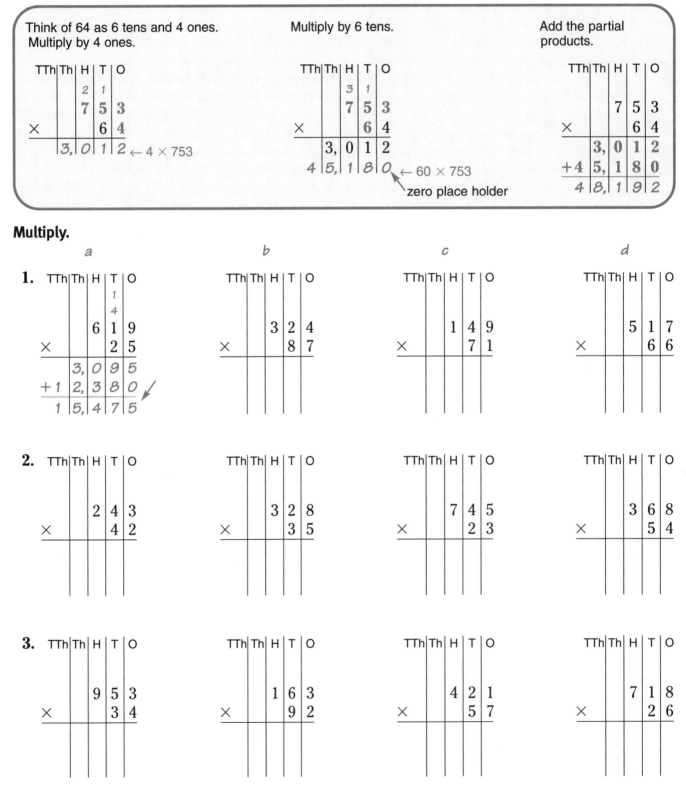

Think of 64 as 6 tens and 4 ones. Multiply by 4 ones.

TTh	Th	H	T	O
		2	1	
		7	5	3
×			6	4
	3,	0	1	2 ← 4 × 753

Multiply by 6 tens.

TTh	Th	H	T	O
		3	1	
		7	5	3
×			6	4
	3,	0	1	2
4	5,	1	8	0 ← 60 × 753

zero place holder

Add the partial products.

TTh	Th	H	T	O
		7	5	3
×			6	4
	3,	0	1	2
+4	5,	1	8	0
4	8,	1	9	2

Multiply.

1.
a.

TTh	Th	H	T	O
			1	
			4	
		6	1	9
×			2	5
	3,	0	9	5
+1	2,	3	8	0
1	5,	4	7	5

b. 324 × 87

c. 149 × 71

d. 517 × 66

2.
a. 243 × 42

b. 328 × 35

c. 745 × 23

d. 368 × 54

3.
a. 953 × 34

b. 163 × 92

c. 421 × 57

d. 718 × 26

Multiply.

	a	b	c	d	e
1.	516×39	277×53	329×61	187×84	917×22
2.	437×24	256×18	704×37	173×45	231×36
3.	532×48	178×29	337×13	540×56	310×81

Line up the digits. Then find the products.

	a	b	c
4.	$631 \times 28 =$ ______	$493 \times 55 =$ ______	$127 \times 86 =$ ______
5.	$237 \times 44 =$ ______	$905 \times 67 =$ ______	

Example for 4a:

$$\begin{array}{r} 631 \\ \times\ 28 \\ \hline \end{array}$$

Estimating Products

To estimate products, round each factor.
Then multiply the rounded factors.

Estimate: 35×72

Round each factor to the greatest place value.
Multiply.

$$\begin{array}{rcrl} 72 & \rightarrow & 70 & \leftarrow \text{2 zeros} \\ \times\ 35 & \rightarrow & \times\ 40 & \\ & & 2,800 & \leftarrow \text{2 zeros} \end{array}$$

Estimate: 719×56

Round each factor to the greatest place value.
Multiply.

$$\begin{array}{rcrl} 719 & \rightarrow & 700 & \leftarrow \text{3 zeros} \\ \times\ 56 & \rightarrow & \times\ 60 & \\ & & 42,000 & \leftarrow \text{3 zeros} \end{array}$$

Estimate the products.

	a	b	c	d
1.	$21 \rightarrow 20$ $\times 29 \rightarrow \times 30$ 600	$44 \rightarrow$ $\times 32 \rightarrow$	$93 \rightarrow$ $\times 14 \rightarrow$	$88 \rightarrow$ $\times 43 \rightarrow$
2.	$79 \rightarrow$ $\times 28 \rightarrow$	$62 \rightarrow$ $\times 61 \rightarrow$	$84 \rightarrow$ $\times 26 \rightarrow$	$76 \rightarrow$ $\times 51 \rightarrow$
3.	$190 \rightarrow$ $\times 38 \rightarrow$	$512 \rightarrow$ $\times 71 \rightarrow$	$664 \rightarrow$ $\times 58 \rightarrow$	$839 \rightarrow$ $\times 24 \rightarrow$

Line up the digits. Then estimate the products.

	a	b	c
4.	34×45 ________ $34 \rightarrow 30$ $\times 45 \rightarrow \times 50$ $1,500$	56×77 ________	768×91 ________

Estimate the products.

	a	b	c	d
1.	$\begin{array}{r} 37 \rightarrow \\ \times 24 \rightarrow \\ \hline \end{array}$	$\begin{array}{r} 55 \rightarrow \\ \times 68 \rightarrow \\ \hline \end{array}$	$\begin{array}{r} 71 \rightarrow \\ \times 17 \rightarrow \\ \hline \end{array}$	$\begin{array}{r} 23 \rightarrow \\ \times 88 \rightarrow \\ \hline \end{array}$
2.	$\begin{array}{r} 42 \rightarrow \\ \times 36 \rightarrow \\ \hline \end{array}$	$\begin{array}{r} 89 \rightarrow \\ \times 54 \rightarrow \\ \hline \end{array}$	$\begin{array}{r} 93 \rightarrow \\ \times 68 \rightarrow \\ \hline \end{array}$	$\begin{array}{r} 99 \rightarrow \\ \times 22 \rightarrow \\ \hline \end{array}$
3.	$\begin{array}{r} 548 \rightarrow \\ \times \quad 45 \rightarrow \\ \hline \end{array}$	$\begin{array}{r} 634 \rightarrow \\ \times \quad 57 \rightarrow \\ \hline \end{array}$	$\begin{array}{r} 178 \rightarrow \\ \times \quad 89 \rightarrow \\ \hline \end{array}$	$\begin{array}{r} 608 \rightarrow \\ \times \quad 91 \rightarrow \\ \hline \end{array}$
4.	$\begin{array}{r} 759 \rightarrow \\ \times \quad 38 \rightarrow \\ \hline \end{array}$	$\begin{array}{r} 214 \rightarrow \\ \times \quad 81 \rightarrow \\ \hline \end{array}$	$\begin{array}{r} 554 \rightarrow \\ \times \quad 47 \rightarrow \\ \hline \end{array}$	$\begin{array}{r} 827 \rightarrow \\ \times \quad 69 \rightarrow \\ \hline \end{array}$

Line up the digits. Then estimate the products.

	a	b	c
5.	27×14 __________ $\begin{array}{r} 27 \rightarrow \\ \times 14 \rightarrow \\ \hline \end{array}$	36×75 __________	63×44 __________
6.	451×36 __________	742×45 __________	494×23 __________

Problem-Solving Method: Make a Table

Chris is ordering new equipment for the football league. He needs to buy 84 helmets, 32 footballs, and 100 team shirts. Footballs cost $24 each. The shirts cost $17 each. The helmets cost $39 each. What will be the total cost for the new equipment?

Understand the problem.

- **What do you want to know?**
  the total cost for the new equipment

- **What information is given?**
  the number and price of each item

Plan how to solve it.

- **What method can you use?**
  You can make a table to organize the information.

Solve it.

- **How can you use this method to solve the problem?**
  Find the total cost for each item. Then add these amounts to find the total cost of all the equipment.

NEW EQUIPMENT				
Equipment	**Number**	**Cost of One**	**Total Cost of Each Item**	
Helmets	84	$39	84 × $39 =	$3,276
Footballs	32	$24	32 × $24 =	$768
Shirts	100	$17	100 × $17 =	$1,700
Total Cost of All the Equipment:				**$5,783**

- **What is the answer?**
  The total cost of all the new equipment is $5,783.

Look back and check your answer.

- **Is your answer reasonable?**
  You can estimate to check your answer.

Helmets:	80 × $40 =	$3,200
Footballs:	30 × $20 =	$600
Shirts:	100 × $20 =	$2,000
		$5,800

The estimate is close to the answer.
The answer is reasonable.

Make a table to solve each problem.

1. On Monday, Sam's Pizza sold 40 large pizzas, 57 mediums, and 35 smalls. A large pizza costs $12. Medium pizzas are $10 each, and small pizzas are $9 each. How much money did Sam's Pizza make on Monday?

Answer ______________________

2. Anya drove 2 hours to get to the train station. Then she rode the train for 14 hours. She drove about 55 miles per hour. The train traveled at about 80 miles per hour. How many miles did Anya travel altogether?

Answer ______________________

3. The dining hall has 25 round tables and 40 square tables. Each round table seats 11 people. Each square table seats 16 people. How many people can sit in the dining hall at the same time?

Answer ______________________

Dividing by 10

To divide by ten, remember that a number divided by one is that number.

Find: 50 ÷ 10

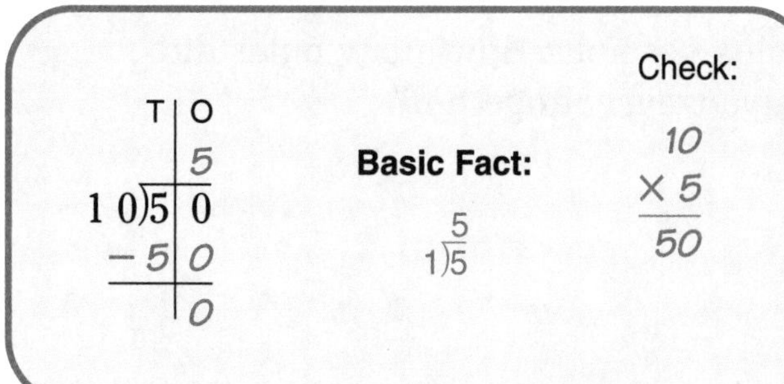

Find: 263 ÷ 10

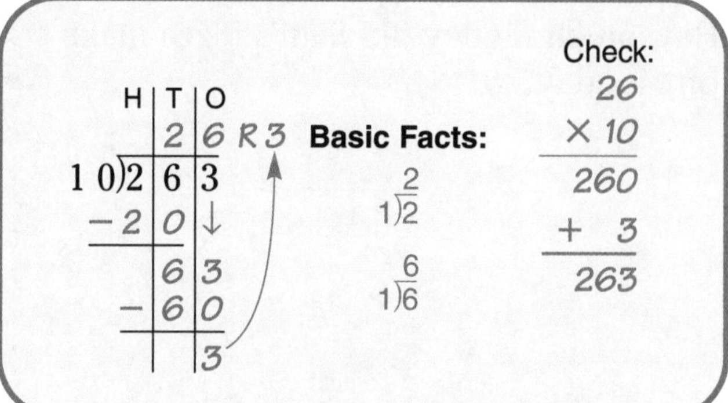

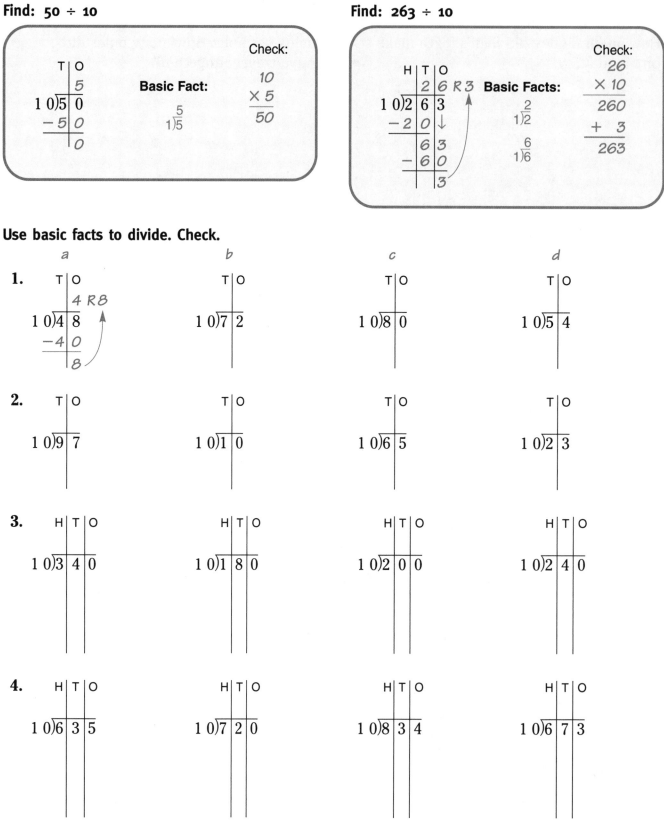

Use basic facts to divide. Check.

	a	b	c	d
1.	10)48 = 4 R8 ($48 - 40 = 8$)	10)72	10)80	10)54
2.	10)97	10)10	10)65	10)23
3.	10)340	10)180	10)200	10)240
4.	10)635	10)720	10)834	10)673

Dividing by Tens

To divide by tens, use basic division facts to choose a trial quotient. Then multiply and subtract.

Find: 90 ÷ 30

To divide, use a basic fact.

	T	O
		3
3 0)	9	0
	−9	0
		0

Basic Fact: $3\overline{)9}$ = 3

Check:

$$\begin{array}{r} 30 \\ \times\ 3 \\ \hline 90 \end{array}$$

Find: 485 ÷ 60

To divide, use a basic fact.

	H	T	O
			8 R5
6 0)	4	8	5
	−4	8	0
			5

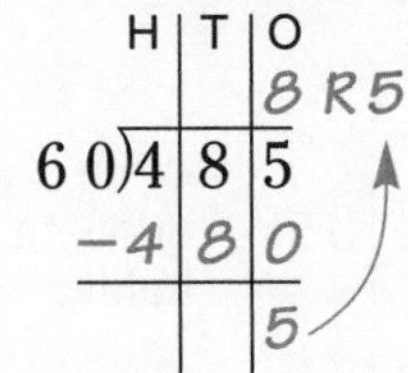

Basic Fact: $6\overline{)48}$ = 8

Check:

$$\begin{array}{r} 60 \\ \times\ 8 \\ \hline 480 \\ +\ \ 5 \\ \hline 485 \end{array}$$

Divide. Check.

	a	b	c	d
1.	$10\overline{)95}$	$30\overline{)90}$	$20\overline{)62}$	$80\overline{)722}$
2.	$50\overline{)300}$	$40\overline{)283}$	$60\overline{)65}$	$70\overline{)6,510}$
3.	$70\overline{)350}$	$30\overline{)1,230}$	$20\overline{)25}$	$50\overline{)100}$
4.	$30\overline{)121}$	$80\overline{)160}$	$10\overline{)36}$	$90\overline{)4,590}$

Set up the problems. Then find the quotients.

	a	b	c
5.	810 ÷ 90 = ________	493 ÷ 70 = ________	120 ÷ 60 = ________

$90\overline{)810}$

Zeros in Quotients

When you cannot divide, write a zero in the quotient as a place holder.

Find: 513 ÷ 5

Divide the hundreds.

H	T	O
1		
5)5	1	3
−5	↓	
0	1	

$5\overline{)5}$ = 1

Divide the tens.

H	T	O
1	0	
5)5	1	3
−5	↓	
0	1	
−	0	↓
	1	3

$5\overline{)1}$ = 0

← Write a zero in the quotient as a place holder.

$1 < 5$

Not enough tens. Bring down the 3 ones.

Divide the ones.

H	T	O
1	0	2 R3
5)5	1	3
−5		
0	1	
−	0	
	1	3
	− 1	0
		3

$5\overline{)13}$ = 2

Check:

$$\begin{array}{r} 102 \\ \times\ 5 \\ \hline 510 \\ +\ 3 \\ \hline 513 \end{array}$$

Divide. Check.

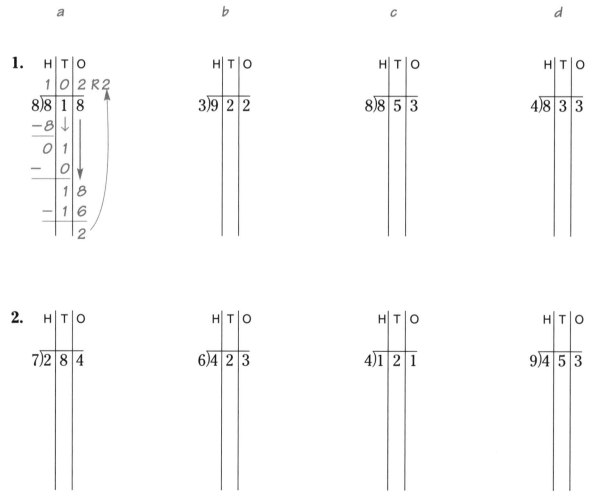

	a	b	c	d
1.	$8\overline{)818}$ = 102 R2	$3\overline{)922}$	$8\overline{)853}$	$4\overline{)833}$
2.	$7\overline{)284}$	$6\overline{)423}$	$4\overline{)121}$	$9\overline{)453}$

Example 1a worked:

H	T	O
1	0	2 R2
8)8	1	8
−8	↓	
0	1	
−	0	↓
	1	8
	− 1	6
		2

Divide. Check.

	a	b	c	d
1.	$3\overline{)303}$	$9\overline{)981}$	$4\overline{)203}$	$6\overline{)485}$
2.	$5\overline{)300}$	$7\overline{)4,930}$	$2\overline{)819}$	$8\overline{)727}$
3.	$9\overline{)278}$	$4\overline{)836}$	$3\overline{)913}$	$2\overline{)1,000}$
4.	$6\overline{)180}$	$5\overline{)3,504}$	$7\overline{)630}$	$8\overline{)3,208}$

Set up the problems. Then find the quotients.

	a	b	c
5.	$240 \div 6 =$ ______	$4,510 \div 5 =$ ______	$361 \div 9 =$ ______
	$6\overline{)240}$		

Trial Quotients: Too Large

When you divide, you may have to try several quotients.

If the product of the trial quotient and the divisor is greater than the dividend, your first trial quotient is too large. Try the number that is 1 less.

Find: 170 ÷ 34

Use rounding to choose a trial quotient.	Try 6 as your trial quotient.	Try 5 as your trial quotient.	Complete the problem.
$34\overline{)173}$	$\begin{array}{r} 6 \\ 34\overline{)173} \\ -204 \end{array}$	$\begin{array}{r} 5 \\ 34\overline{)173} \\ -170 \end{array}$	$\begin{array}{r} 5\text{ R}3 \\ 34\overline{)173} \\ -170 \\ 3 \end{array}$
Think: 34 rounds to 30. 170 rounds to 200. $3\overline{)20}$ = 6 So, $34\overline{)200}$ = 6.	Since 204 > 173, 6 is too large.	Since 170 < 173, 5 is correct.	

Write *too large* or *correct* for each trial quotient.

	a		b		c	
1.	$\begin{array}{r} 2 \\ 31\overline{)608} \\ -62 \end{array}$	too large	$\begin{array}{r} 7 \\ 43\overline{)329} \end{array}$	________	$\begin{array}{r} 3 \\ 53\overline{)1,573} \end{array}$	________
2.	$\begin{array}{r} 2 \\ 42\overline{)8,190} \end{array}$	________	$\begin{array}{r} 2 \\ 12\overline{)239} \end{array}$	________	$\begin{array}{r} 5 \\ 76\overline{)421} \end{array}$	________
3.	$\begin{array}{r} 7 \\ 33\overline{)2,395} \end{array}$	________	$\begin{array}{r} 2 \\ 63\overline{)1,846} \end{array}$	________	$\begin{array}{r} 5 \\ 72\overline{)3,598} \end{array}$	________

Trial Quotients: Too Small

If the difference between the dividend and the product of the trial quotient and divisor is greater than or equal to the divisor, your first trial quotient is too small. Try the number that is 1 greater.

Find: 527 ÷ 17

Use rounding to choose a trial quotient.	Try 2 as your trial quotient.	Try 3 as your trial quotient.	Complete the problem.
$17\overline{)527}$	$\begin{array}{r} 2 \\ 17\overline{)527} \\ -34 \\ \hline 18 \end{array}$	$\begin{array}{r} 3 \\ 17\overline{)527} \\ -51 \\ \hline 1 \end{array}$	$\begin{array}{r} 31 \\ 17\overline{)527} \\ -51\downarrow \\ \hline 17 \\ -17 \\ \hline 0 \end{array}$
Think: 17 rounds to 20. 527 rounds to 500. $\overset{2}{2\overline{)5}}$ So, $\overset{2}{17\overline{)52}}$.	Since 18 > 17, 2 is too small.	Since 1 < 17, 3 is correct.	

Write *too small* or *correct* for each trial quotient.

	a		b		c	
1.	$\begin{array}{r} 5 \\ 28\overline{)168} \\ -140 \\ \hline 28 \end{array}$	too small	$\begin{array}{r} 8 \\ 12\overline{)960} \end{array}$	________	$\begin{array}{r} 4 \\ 18\overline{)930} \end{array}$	________
2.	$\begin{array}{r} 1 \\ 26\overline{)5,486} \end{array}$	________	$\begin{array}{r} 4 \\ 57\overline{)2,859} \end{array}$	________	$\begin{array}{r} 5 \\ 78\overline{)390} \end{array}$	________
3.	$\begin{array}{r} 3 \\ 39\overline{)1,560} \end{array}$	________	$\begin{array}{r} 5 \\ 46\overline{)2,760} \end{array}$	________	$\begin{array}{r} 2 \\ 83\overline{)1,743} \end{array}$	________

Two-digit Divisors

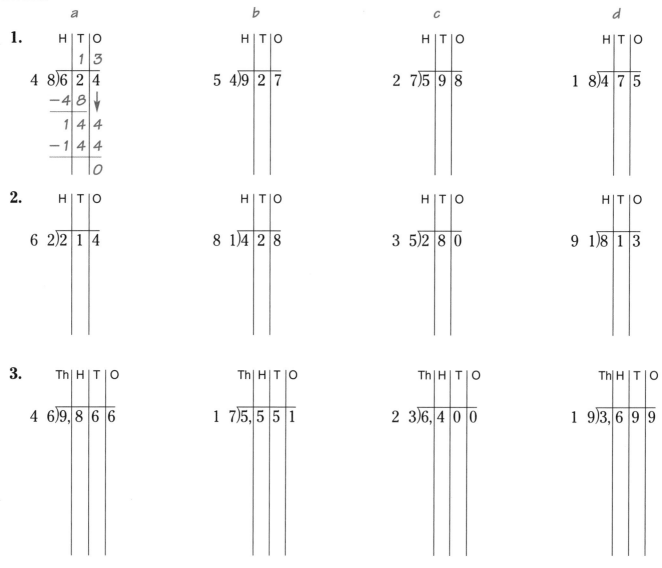

To divide by a two-digit divisor, first choose a trial quotient. Then multiply and subtract.

Find: 889 ÷ 34

Choose a trial quotient.

H | T | O

$34\overline{)889}$

Think: $3\overline{)8}$ is 2. So, $34\overline{)88}$ is about 2.

Multiply and subtract.

H | T | O

2

$34\overline{)889}$
−68
209

Think: $3\overline{)20}$ is 6. So, $34\overline{)209}$ is about 6.

Multiply and subtract.

H | T | O

26 R5

$34\overline{)889}$
−68
209
−204
5

Check:

26
×34
884
+5
889

Divide.

1.

a. H | T | O

13

$48\overline{)624}$
−48
144
−144
0

b. $54\overline{)927}$

c. $27\overline{)598}$

d. $18\overline{)475}$

2.

a. $62\overline{)214}$

b. $81\overline{)428}$

c. $35\overline{)280}$

d. $91\overline{)813}$

3.

a. $46\overline{)9{,}866}$

b. $17\overline{)5{,}551}$

c. $23\overline{)6{,}400}$

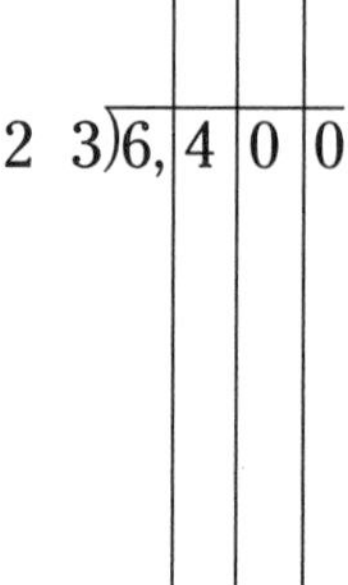

d. $19\overline{)3{,}699}$

Divide.

	a	b	c	d
1.	$38\overline{)244}$	$28\overline{)168}$	$14\overline{)812}$	$39\overline{)591}$
2.	$55\overline{)781}$	$32\overline{)608}$	$19\overline{)270}$	$15\overline{)930}$
3.	$63\overline{)4,815}$	$83\overline{)4,648}$	$42\overline{)8,190}$	$44\overline{)5,566}$
4.	$76\overline{)4,104}$	$91\overline{)3,076}$	$68\overline{)2,439}$	$85\overline{)7,240}$
5.	$24\overline{)4,008}$	$53\overline{)1,584}$	$13\overline{)1,671}$	$25\overline{)7,855}$

Set up the problems. Then find the quotients.

	a	b	c
6.	$886 \div 74 =$ ________ $74\overline{)886}$	$187 \div 22 =$ ________	$645 \div 49 =$ ________
7.	$6{,}409 \div 37 =$ ________	$7{,}298 \div 36 =$ ________	$7{,}545 \div 52 =$ ________

Estimating Quotients

To estimate quotients, round the numbers until you are able to use a basic fact.

Estimate: 237 ÷ 6

Round the dividend to use a basic fact. Divide.

$6\overline{)237}$

$237 \div 6$
$\downarrow \quad \downarrow$
$240 \div 6 = 40$

Think: $24 \div 6 = 4$

Estimate: 418 ÷ 72

Round the dividend and the divisor to use a basic fact. Divide.

$73\overline{)418}$

$418 \div 73$
$\downarrow \quad \downarrow$
$420 \div 70 = 6$

Think: $42 \div 7 = 6$

Round the dividends to estimate the quotients.

	a	*b*	*c*	*d*
1.	$152 \div 4$ $\downarrow \quad \downarrow$ *160 ÷ 4 = 40*	$248 \div 5$ $\downarrow \quad \downarrow$	$627 \div 7$ $\downarrow \quad \downarrow$	$825 \div 9$ $\downarrow \quad \downarrow$
2.	$5{,}432 \div 8$ $\downarrow \quad \downarrow$	$2{,}651 \div 3$ $\downarrow \quad \downarrow$	$1{,}755 \div 6$ $\downarrow \quad \downarrow$	$4{,}859 \div 7$ $\downarrow \quad \downarrow$

Round the dividends and the divisors to estimate the quotients.

	a	*b*	*c*	*d*
3.	$345 \div 52$ $\downarrow \quad \downarrow$ *350 ÷ 50 = 7*	$183 \div 89$ $\downarrow \quad \downarrow$	$778 \div 38$ $\downarrow \quad \downarrow$	$845 \div 19$ $\downarrow \quad \downarrow$
4.	$2{,}417 \div 82$ $\downarrow \quad \downarrow$	$1{,}212 \div 21$ $\downarrow \quad \downarrow$	$3{,}219 \div 39$ $\downarrow \quad \downarrow$	$5{,}583 \div 94$ $\downarrow \quad \downarrow$

Round the dividends to estimate the quotients.

	a	b	c
1.	$4\overline{)358} \rightarrow \overset{90}{4\overline{)360}}$	$3\overline{)241} \rightarrow$	$7\overline{)207} \rightarrow$
2.	$8\overline{)402} \rightarrow$	$6\overline{)363} \rightarrow$	$5\overline{)346} \rightarrow$
3.	$2\overline{)1,132} \rightarrow$	$4\overline{)2,713} \rightarrow$	$9\overline{)5,534} \rightarrow$

Round the dividends and the divisors to estimate the quotients.

	a	b	c
4.	$53\overline{)465} \rightarrow \overset{90}{50\overline{)450}}$	$31\overline{)866} \rightarrow$	$58\overline{)295} \rightarrow$
5.	$24\overline{)158} \rightarrow$	$43\overline{)824} \rightarrow$	$87\overline{)275} \rightarrow$
6.	$28\overline{)6,017} \rightarrow$	$94\overline{)3,481} \rightarrow$	$49\overline{)2,807} \rightarrow$

Problem-Solving Method: Complete a Pattern

In 1999, Old Faithful Geyser in Yellowstone National Park had about 56,000 visitors a week. About how many people visited each day?

Understand the problem.

- **What do you want to know?**
  about how many visitors there were each day

- **What information do you know?**
  56,000 people visited each week.
  There are 7 days in a week.

Plan how to solve it.

- **What method can you use?**
  You can find and complete a pattern.

Solve it.

- **How can you use this method to solve the problem?**
  Start with a basic division fact. Then use a pattern of zeros to find 56,000 ÷ 7.

$$
\begin{array}{llll}
56 & \div 7 & = 8 & \leftarrow \text{Basic Fact} \\
560 & \div 7 & = 80 & \\
5{,}600 & \div 7 & = 800 & \\
56{,}000 & \div 7 & = 8{,}000 & \leftarrow \text{Zero Pattern} \\
\uparrow & & \uparrow & \\
\text{three zeros} & & \text{three zeros} &
\end{array}
$$

- **What is the answer?**
  About 8,000 people visited Old Faithful every day.

Look back and check your answer.

- **Is your answer reasonable?**
  You can check your division with multiplication.

$$
\begin{array}{r}
8{,}000 \\
\times \quad 7 \\
\hline
56{,}000
\end{array}
$$

The product matches the dividend. The answer is reasonable.

Complete a pattern to solve each problem.

1. The stadium has 48,000 seats. The seats are divided into 80 sections. How many seats are in each section?

48	÷	**8**	=	**6**
480	÷	**80**	=	**6**
4,800	÷	**80**	=	**60**
48,000	÷	**80**	=	_____

   Answer ____________________

2. The theater collected $2,700 at the box office last night. If they sold 90 tickets, how much did each ticket cost?

27	÷	**9**	=	**3**
270	÷	**90**	=	**3**
2,700	÷	**90**	=	_____

   Answer ____________________

3. The average human heart rate is 4,200 beats per hour. About how many times does a human heart beat per minute? (1 hour = 60 minutes)

42	÷	**6**	=	**7**
420	÷	**60**	=	**7**
4,200	÷	**60**	=	_____

   Answer ____________________

4. In 1999, the Empire State Building had about 21,000 visitors each week. About how many people visited each day? (1 week = 7 days)

21	÷	**7**	=	**3**
210	÷	**7**	=	**30**
2,100	÷	**7**	=	**300**
21,000	÷	**7**	=	_____

   Answer ____________________

5. The factory has 40 trucks to deliver 3,600 computers. How many computers will each truck deliver?

36	÷	**4**	=	_____
360	÷	**40**	=	_____
3,600	÷	**40**	=	_____

   Answer ____________________

6. A passenger helicopter can fly 3,000 miles in 10 hours. What is the average speed of the helicopter?

3	÷	**1**	=	_____
30	÷	**10**	=	_____
300	÷	**10**	=	_____
3,000	÷	**10**	=	_____

   Answer ____________________

Problem Solving

Solve.

1. In 10 hours, Noriko drove her car 520 miles. She drove the same number of miles each hour. How many miles did she travel each hour?

Answer ______________________

2. The lodge members collected 840 cans of food. They put 24 cans in each box. How many boxes did they fill?

Answer ______________________

3. Dale spends $5,832 each year on rent. He pays the same amount each month. How much are his monthly payments?

Answer ______________________

4. Angelo's Bakery sold 4,123 pies in July. How many pies did they sell during an average day? (There are 31 days in July.)

Answer ______________________

5. One of the tallest buildings in the world is the Petronas Tower in Malaysia. It is 1,483 feet tall and has 88 stories. Estimate how tall each story is.

Answer ______________________

6. Kay has 486 beads. She plans to use 35 beads for each necklace. How many necklaces can she make? How many beads will she have left over?

Answer ______________________

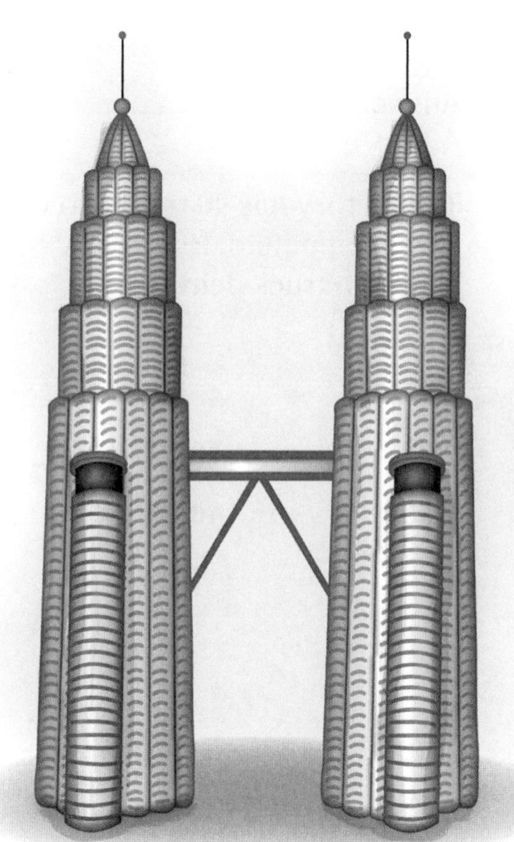

UNIT 5 Review

Multiply. Check.

	a	b	c	d
1.	40×9	7×40	100×8	6×100
2.	17×34	85×52	48×23	89×67
3.	135×24	862×19	403×58	683×41

Set up the problems. Then find the products.

	a	b	c
4.	$37 \times 45 =$ ______	$68 \times 19 =$ ______	$94 \times 56 =$ ______
5.	$394 \times 22 =$ ______	$708 \times 64 =$ ______	$589 \times 37 =$ ______

Estimate the products.

	a	b	c	d
6.	$49 \rightarrow$ $\times 22 \rightarrow$	$57 \rightarrow$ $\times 38 \rightarrow$	$184 \rightarrow$ $\times 67 \rightarrow$	$269 \rightarrow$ $\times 83 \rightarrow$

UNIT 5 Review

Divide. Check.

	a	b	c	d
7.	$10\overline{)85}$	$20\overline{)600}$	$30\overline{)69}$	$70\overline{)5{,}615}$
8.	$9\overline{)181}$	$7\overline{)774}$	$6\overline{)1{,}234}$	$8\overline{)2{,}464}$
9.	$47\overline{)235}$	$24\overline{)1{,}176}$	$63\overline{)6{,}450}$	$79\overline{)4{,}938}$

Set up the problems. Then find the quotients.

	a	b	c
10.	$511 \div 36 =$ __________	$614 \div 28 =$ __________	$4{,}368 \div 81 =$ __________

Write *too large*, *too small*, or *correct* for each trial quotient.

	a	b	c
11.	$\begin{array}{r} 6 \\ 34\overline{)195} \end{array}$	$\begin{array}{r} 5 \\ 65\overline{)4{,}041} \end{array}$	$\begin{array}{r} 7 \\ 29\overline{)2{,}295} \end{array}$
	__________	__________	__________

Estimate the quotients by rounding each number until you can use a basic fact.

	a	b	c	d
12.	$637 \div 8$	$4{,}863 \div 7$	$567 \div 74$	$1{,}786 \div 89$
	↓ ↓	↓ ↓	↓ ↓	↓ ↓

Make a table to solve each problem.

13. Bill sold 28 large T-shirts, 42 mediums, and 17 smalls. A large T-shirt costs $18. Medium T-shirts are $16 each, and small T-shirts are $12 each. How much money did Bill make for all the T-shirts he sold?

Answer ____________________

14. Jane bought 13 packs of plates, 25 packs of cups, and 8 packs of napkins. There are 80 plates in each pack, 40 cups in each pack, and 100 napkins in each pack. Which item does she have the most of?

Answer ____________________

Find and complete a pattern to solve each problem.

15. A frog's heart beats 1,800 times per hour. About how many times does a frog's heart beat per minute? (1 hour = 60 minutes)

Answer ____________________

16. In 1999, the London Tower in England got about 49,000 visitors each week. About how many people visited each day?

Answer ____________________

17. The telethon collected $6,400 yesterday in $80 pledges. How many people pledged $80 each?

Answer ____________________

Unit 6
Time, Money, and Measurement

Time

A **day** is divided into **hours, minutes,** and **seconds**.
Both of these clocks show the same time of day.

Write: 2:35

Read: 35 minutes after 2 or 25 minutes before 3

1 day = 24 hours
1 hour = 60 minutes
1 minute = 60 seconds

You can multiply or divide to change units of time.

To change larger units to smaller units, multiply.	To change smaller units to larger units, divide.
8 hours = *480* minutes	180 seconds = *3* minutes
8 × 60 = 480	180 ÷ 60 = 3
total hours × minutes in one hour	total seconds ÷ seconds in one minute

Write the time shown on each clock.

1.

4:45 ______

______

______

______

Change the units of time.

	a	*b*
2.	120 minutes = ______ hours	4 minutes = ______ seconds
3.	10 hours = ______ minutes	5 days = ______ hours
4.	144 hours = ______ days	540 seconds = ______ minutes
5.	20 days = ______ hours	half hour = ______ minutes

Calendar

A year is divided into **months, weeks,** and **days**.
The **calendar** below shows the 365 days in the year 2001.

CALENDAR FOR THE YEAR 2001			
JANUARY	FEBRUARY	MARCH	APRIL
S M T W T F S	S M T W T F S	S M T W T F S	S M T W T F S
1 2 3 4 5 6 7 8 9 10 11 12 13 14 15 16 17 18 19 20 21 22 23 24 25 26 27 28 29 30 31	1 2 3 4 5 6 7 8 9 10 11 12 13 14 15 16 17 18 19 20 21 22 23 24 25 26 27 28	1 2 3 4 5 6 7 8 9 10 11 12 13 14 15 16 17 18 19 20 21 22 23 24 25 26 27 28 29 30 31	1 2 3 4 5 6 7 8 9 10 11 12 13 14 15 16 17 18 19 20 21 22 23 24 25 26 27 28 29 30
MAY	JUNE	JULY	AUGUST
S M T W T F S	S M T W T F S	S M T W T F S	S M T W T F S
1 2 3 4 5 6 7 8 9 10 11 12 13 14 15 16 17 18 19 20 21 22 23 24 25 26 27 28 29 30 31	1 2 3 4 5 6 7 8 9 10 11 12 13 14 15 16 17 18 19 20 21 22 23 24 25 26 27 28 29 30	1 2 3 4 5 6 7 8 9 10 11 12 13 14 15 16 17 18 19 20 21 22 23 24 25 26 27 28 29 30 31	1 2 3 4 5 6 7 8 9 10 11 12 13 14 15 16 17 18 19 20 21 22 23 24 25 26 27 28 29 30 31
SEPTEMBER	OCTOBER	NOVEMBER	DECEMBER
S M T W T F S	S M T W T F S	S M T W T F S	S M T W T F S
1 2 3 4 5 6 7 8 9 10 11 12 13 14 15 16 17 18 19 20 21 22 23 24 25 26 27 28 29 30	1 2 3 4 5 6 7 8 9 10 11 12 13 14 15 16 17 18 19 20 21 22 23 24 25 26 27 28 29 30 31	1 2 3 4 5 6 7 8 9 10 11 12 13 14 15 16 17 18 19 20 21 22 23 24 25 26 27 28 29 30	1 2 3 4 5 6 7 8 9 10 11 12 13 14 15 16 17 18 19 20 21 22 23 24 25 26 27 28 29 30 31

7 days = 1 week
52 weeks = 1 year
12 months = 1 year

Use the calendar to write each day and date.

a | *b*

1. 2 days after November 12, 2001 — *Wednesday, November 14, 2001* ______ | 5 days before April 1, 2001 ______

2. the third Tuesday in February, 2001 ______ | 2 weeks after July 4, 2001 ______

3. 1 week before December 5, 2001 ______ | 3 days after the last Monday in May, 2001 ______

Change the units of time.

a | *b*

4. 7 days = *168* hours | 48 months = ______ years

5. 3 weeks = ______ days | 2 years = ______ days

6. 112 days = ______ weeks | 15 years = ______ months

7. 3 years = ______ weeks | 84 days = ______ weeks

Elapsed Time

Elapsed time is the amount of time that passes from the start of an event to its end.

These clocks show that 3 hours and 15 minutes elapse between 8:00 and 11:15.

Start

End

You can add or subtract elapsed time.

To find when an event ended, add.		To find when an event started, subtract.	
Start Time → 8:00	8 hr 0 min	End Time → 11:15	11 hr 15 min
+ Elapsed Time →	+ 3 hr 15 min	− Elapsed Time →	− 3 hr 15 min
End Time → 11:15	11 hr 15 min	Start Time → 8:00	8 hr 0 min

Tell how much time has elapsed.

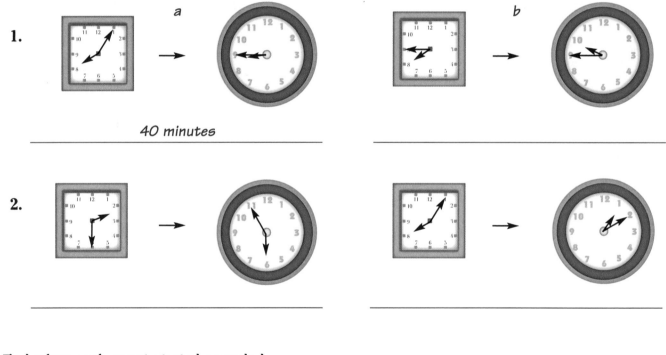

a | *b*

1.  → 

40 minutes

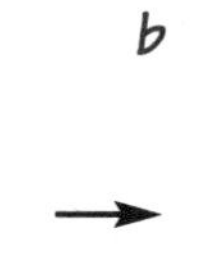 → 

______

2.  → 

______

→ 

______

Find when each event started or ended.

a

3. Start: 7:10 — 7 hr 10 min

Elapsed Time: 1 hr 15 min — + 1 hr 15 min

______

b

End: 10:30 — 10 hr 30 min

Elapsed Time: 3 hr 5 min — − 3 hr 5 min

______

Using a Schedule

A **schedule** is a list or table showing when events happen.

FLIGHT SCHEDULE from CHICAGO, ILLINOIS		
Destination	**Departs**	**Arrives**
New Orleans, Louisiana	7:15	10:45
Houston, Texas	9:00	11:35
Birmingham, Alabama	2:30	4:05
Jackson, Mississippi	3:20	5:35
Kansas City, Missouri	6:00	7:20
Little Rock, Arkansas	8:00	9:35

Use the flight schedule to find each answer.

	a	*b*
1.	How long is the flight from Chicago to Houston? *2 hours and 35 minutes*	How long is the flight from Chicago to Little Rock? __________
2.	How long is the flight from Chicago to New Orleans? __________	How long is the flight from Chicago to Birmingham? __________
3.	How long is the flight from Chicago to Jackson? __________	How long is the flight from Chicago to Kansas City? __________
4.	Which is the shortest flight on the schedule? __________	Which is the longest flight on the schedule? __________
5.	If it takes 60 minutes to check in for a flight, what time should you arrive at the airport for the flight to Houston? __________	If it takes 30 minutes to drive to the airport, what time should you leave to meet the flight when it arrives in New Orleans? __________

Money

To write money amounts, use a **decimal point**, or period, to separate dollars and cents.
A **decimal** is a number less than 1.

> **four dollars and sixteen cents**
> ↓
> **$4.16**

These coins are each worth less than 1 dollar.

penny
1¢ or $0.01

nickel
5¢ or $0.05

dime
10¢ or $0.10

quarter
25¢ or $0.25

half-dollar
50¢ or $0.50

These bills are each worth 1 dollar or more.

1 dollar
$1 or $1.00

5 dollars
$5 or $5.00

10 dollars
$10 or $10.00

Answer each question. Remember, 1 dollar = 100 cents.

	a	*b*
1.	1 dollar = __100__ pennies	1 dollar = ______ nickels
2.	1 dollar = ______ dimes	1 dollar = ______ quarters
3.	1 dollar = ______ half-dollars	$5.00 = ______ dollars
4.	$10.00 = ______ dollars	$0.30 = ______ dimes
5.	$0.55 = ______ nickels	$1.25 = ______ quarters

Write each money amount using digits.

	a	*b*
6.	two dollars and thirty cents __$2.30__	seven dollars and forty cents ______
7.	nine cents ______	ten dollars and sixty-one cents ______
8.	eighteen dollars ______	thirteen dollars and two cents ______
9.	3 nickels and 4 pennies ______	2 quarters and 4 dimes ______

Add and Subtract Money

Add and subtract money the same way as whole numbers.
First line up the decimal points. Add or subtract.
Then place the decimal point and **dollar sign** in the answer.

Find: $0.25 + $1.15

Line up the decimal points.	Add. Write your answer in dollars and cents.
\$ 0.2 5 + 1.1 5	\$ 0.2 5 + 1.1 5 \$ 1.4 0

Find: $1.00 – $0.25

Line up the decimal points.	Subtract. Write your answer in dollars and cents.
\$ 1.0 0 − 0.2 5	0 9 10 \$ 1.0 0 − 0.2 5 \$ 0.7 5

Add.

	a	*b*	*c*	*d*
1.	\$ 0.2 5 + 0.3 1 \$0.5 6	\$ 0.5 4 + 0.2 9	\$ 0.2 8 + 1.3 6	\$ 1.2 9 + 0.5 2
2.	\$ 2.1 9 + 5.1 4	\$ 2.2 6 + 3.1 7	\$ 4.2 5 + 3.3 5	\$ 2 2.5 0 + 1 4.0 7

Subtract.

	a	*b*	*c*	*d*
3.	\$ 0.9 9 − 0.4 5 \$0.5 4	\$ 0.2 7 − 0.1 4	\$ 2.6 5 − 1.4 0	\$ 2 0.4 8 − 1 0.3 5
4.	\$ 0.7 2 − 0.2 3	\$ 0.9 2 − 0.4 7	\$ 4.3 5 − 2.4 8	\$ 5.5 7 − 2.7 9

Multiply and Divide Money

Multiply and divide money the same as whole numbers.
To multiply, first set up the problem. Multiply or divide.
Then place the decimal point and dollar sign in the answer.

Find: $5.42 × 3

Set up the problem.

$$\begin{array}{r} \$\,5.42 \\ \times \quad 3 \\ \hline \end{array}$$

Multiply. Write your answer in dollars and cents.

$$\begin{array}{r} \$\,5.42 \\ \times \quad 3 \\ \hline \$16.26 \end{array}$$

Find: $2.10 ÷ 3

Set up the problem.

$3\overline{)\$\,2.10}$

Divide. Write your answer in dollars and cents.

$$\begin{array}{r} \$0.70 \\ 3\overline{)\$2.10} \\ -2.1 \\ \hline 00 \end{array}$$

Check.

$$\begin{array}{r} {}^{2} \\ \$\,0.70 \\ \times \quad 3 \\ \hline \$2.10 \end{array}$$

Multiply.

	a	b	c	d
1.	$2.21 × 7 = $15.47	$2.32 × 4	$4.51 × 5	$1.06 × 8
2.	$1.10 × 25	$2.12 × 14	$1.25 × 30	$2.07 × 11

Divide.

3.	$4\overline{)\$\,2.48}$	$5\overline{)\$\,3.50}$	$8\overline{)\$\,4.00}$	$6\overline{)\$\,3.72}$
4.	$9\overline{)\$\,3.60}$	$7\overline{)\$\,42.00}$	$6\overline{)\$\,36.12}$	$4\overline{)\$\,0.84}$

Problem-Solving Method: Work Backwards

Maggie had $9.25 left over after going to the State Fair. Admission was $12.50. She spent $18.75 on ride tickets and bought a funnel cake for $2.50. How much money did she take to the fair?

Understand the problem.

- **What do you want to know?**
  how much money Maggie took to the fair

- **What information is given?**
  She spent $12.50 to get in, $18.75 for rides, and $2.50 for food. She had $9.25 left over.

Plan how to solve it.

- **What method can you use?**
  You can work backwards. Work from the amount she had left to find the amount she started with.

Solve it.

- **How can you use this method to solve the problem?**
  Addition is the opposite of subtraction. So, add the amounts she spent to the amount she had left over.

$ 9.25	← amount left over
12.50	← admission
18.75	← ride tickets
+ 2.50	← funnel cake
$43.00	

- **What is the answer?**
  Maggie took $43.00 to the State Fair.

Look back and check your answer.

- **Is your answer reasonable?**
  You can check by working forwards. Subtract the amounts she spent from the amount she took to the fair.

$$\begin{array}{r} \$43.00 \\ -\ 12.50 \\ \hline \$30.50 \\ -\ 18.75 \\ \hline \$11.75 \\ -\ 2.50 \\ \hline \$\ 9.25 \end{array}$$

The amounts left over match. The answer is reasonable.

Work backwards to solve each problem.

1. Juan had $9.45 left over after going to the movies. He spent $7.50 for his ticket. Then he bought popcorn for $3.75 and a drink for $2.35. How much money did he start with?

Answer ____________________

2. Craig gave the cashier $50 to pay for 4 CDs. His change was $2.00. How much did each CD cost?

Answer ____________________

3. Soccer practice ended at 7:00. The team stretched for 10 minutes and practiced for 40 minutes. Then they played a game for 35 minutes. What time did the soccer practice start?

Answer ____________________

4. Latoya got home from shopping at 4:30. She spent 1 hour and 15 minutes at the mall. Then she did her grocery shopping for 30 minutes. What time did she start shopping?

Answer ____________________

5. Naomi has $35.00 left over from her paycheck after paying bills. Her rent is $450.00 and her car insurance is $85.25. She spent $46.81 on groceries. How much is her paycheck?

Answer ____________________

Customary Units

Measure Length

1 foot (ft.) = 12 inches (in.)
1 yard (yd.) = 3 ft.
1 mile (mi.) = 5,280 ft.

One inch is this long. 1 in.

This page is about 1 foot long.

A door is about 1 yard wide.

A mile is about the distance you can walk in 20 minutes.

Measure Weight

1 pound (lb.) = 16 ounces (oz.)
1 ton (T.) = 2,000 pounds

A slice of bread weighs about 1 ounce.

A box of cereal weighs about 1 pound.

A truck weighs about 1 ton.

Measure Capacity

1 pint (pt.) = 2 cups (c.)
1 quart (qt.) = 2 pt.
1 gallon (gal.) = 4 qt.

A school milk carton holds 1 cup.

A small container of ice cream holds 1 pint.

A small saucepan holds about 1 quart.

A large jug of milk holds 1 gallon.

Choose the most appropriate unit of measure. Write *in.*, *ft.*, or *mi.*

	a	b
1.	length of your finger ___in.___	height of a flagpole ______
2.	width of a room ______	length of Lake Erie ______

Choose the most appropriate unit of measure. Write *oz.*, *lb.*, or *T.*

	a	b
3.	weight of a dog ___lb.___	weight of a truckload of coal ______
4.	weight of a ship ______	weight of a comb ______

Choose the most appropriate unit of measure. Write *c.*, *pt.*, *qt.*, or *gal.*

	a	b
5.	capacity of a coffee mug ___c.___	capacity of a bathtub ______
6.	capacity of a container of yogurt ______	capacity of a baby bottle ______

Change the units of measure.

	a	b	c
7.	2 lb. = ___32___ oz.	2,000 lb. = ______ T.	32 oz. = ______ lb.
8.	3 yd. = ______ ft.	5,280 ft. = ______ mi.	6 ft. = ______ in.
9.	4 pt. = ______ qt.	6 c. = ______ pt.	5 gal. = ______ qt.

Metric Units

Measure Length

1 meter (m) = 100 centimeters (cm) 1 kilometer (km) = 1,000 meters

One centimeter is this long. 1 cm

A baseball bat is about 1 meter long.

A kilometer is about the distance you can walk in 15 minutes.

Measure Weight

1 kilogram (kg) = 1,000 grams (g)

A paper clip weighs about 1 gram.

A dictionary weighs about 1 kilogram.

Measure Capacity

1 liter (L) = 1,000 milliliters (mL)

An eyedropper holds about 1 milliliter.

A large bottle of soda holds 2 liters.

Choose the most appropriate unit of measure. Write *cm*, *m*, or *km*.

	a	*b*
1.	distance between airports *km*	height of a giraffe ______
2.	width of a doorway ______	length of a toothbrush ______

Choose the most appropriate unit of measure. Write *g* or *kg*.

	a	*b*
3.	weight of a notebook *kg*	weight of a feather ______
4.	weight of a penny ______	weight of a football ______

Choose the most appropriate unit of measure. Write *mL* or *L*.

	a	*b*
5.	capacity of a baby bottle *mL*	capacity of a juice glass ______
6.	capacity of a kitchen sink ______	capacity of a spoon ______

Change the units of measure.

	a	*b*	*c*
7.	3 L = *3,000* mL	500 cm = ______ m	2 kg = ______ g
8.	4 km = ______ m	8,000 g = ______ kg	5 L = ______ mL
9.	10 m = ______ cm	6,000 mL = ______ L	1,000 cm = ______ m

Comparing Units of Measurement

To compare two measurements, first try to change them to the same unit.

Remember, to change larger units to smaller units, multiply.

Compare: 2 m to 300 cm

Think: 1 m = 100 cm
2 m = 2 × 100 = 200 cm

200 cm *is less than* 300 cm

2m < 300 cm

Compare: 15 qt. to 3 gal.

Think: 1 gal. = 4 qt.
3 gal. = 3 × 4 = 12 qt.

15 qt. *is greater than* 12 qt.

15 qt. > 3 gal.

Compare. Write <, >, or =.

	a	*b*	*c*
1.	48 in. *=* 4 ft.	3,500 g ______ 4 kg	500 mm ______ 5 cm
	1 ft. = 12 in. *4 ft. = 4 × 12 = 48 in.*		
2.	3 km ______ 2,000 m	2 T. ______ 4,000 lb.	40,000 mL ______ 40 L
3.	12 ft. ______ 5 yd.	6 pt. ______ 10 c.	5 ft. ______ 600 in.
4.	2 mi. ______ 5,280 ft.	10 m ______ 1,000 cm	7 gal. ______ 30 qt.
5.	3 km ______ 2,000 m	5 T. ______ 500 lb.	8,000 g ______ 80 kg
6.	30 qt. ______ 5 gal.	10 km ______ 10,000 m	40 yd. ______ 120 ft.
7.	6 ft. ______ 100 in.	48 oz. ______ 2 lb.	9 L ______ 9,000 mL

Problem-Solving Method: Use a Graph

Devon is planning a trip to Seattle, Washington sometime between October and February. He found this graph on the Internet. He wants to pick the least rainy time to go. In which month should he go to Seattle?

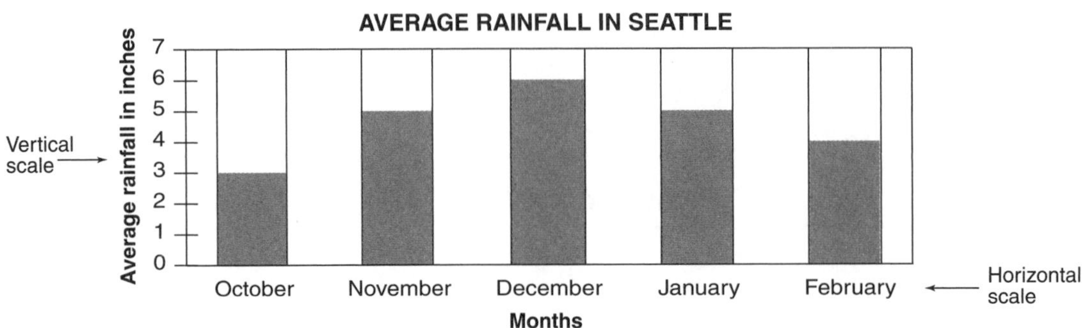

Understand the problem.

- **What do you want to know?**
  the least rainy time between October and February to visit Seattle

- **What information is given?**
  a bar graph showing the average monthly rainfall in Seattle

Plan how to solve it.

- **What method can you use?**
  You can use the bar graph to compare the data.

Solve it.

- **How can you use this method to solve the problem?**
  Compare the lengths of the bars for each month. The month with the shortest bar has the least rainfall.

- **What is the answer?**
  Devon should plan his trip for October.

Look back and check your answer.

- **Is your answer reasonable?**
  You can find the number of inches of rain for each month on the vertical scale of the graph and compare.

Oct. = 3 in.
Nov. = 5 in.
Dec. = 6 in.
Jan. = 5 in.
Feb. = 4 in.

October has the least average rainfall, 3 inches.
The answer is reasonable.

Use the graphs to solve each problem.

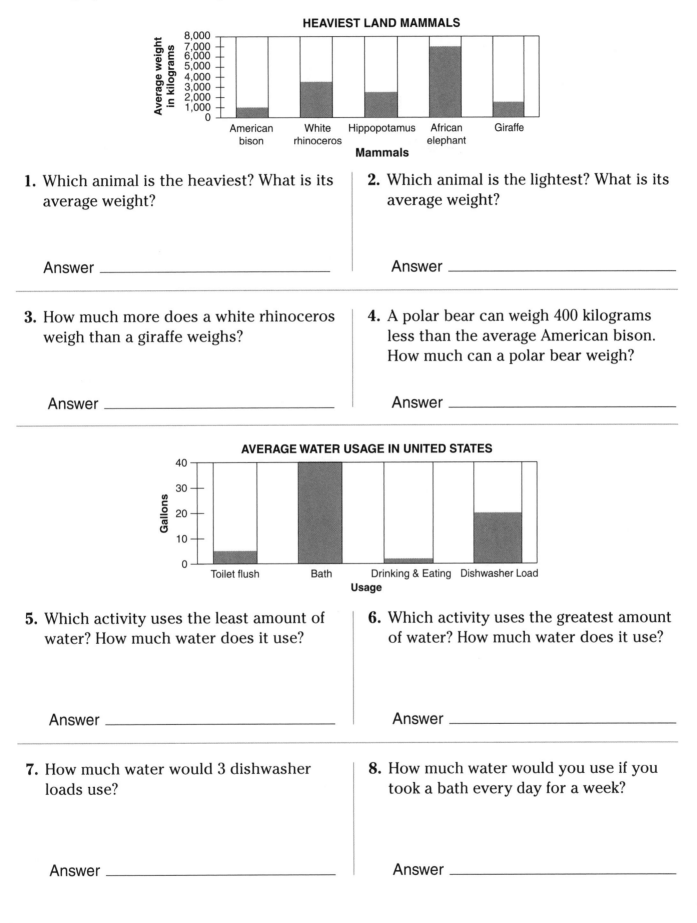

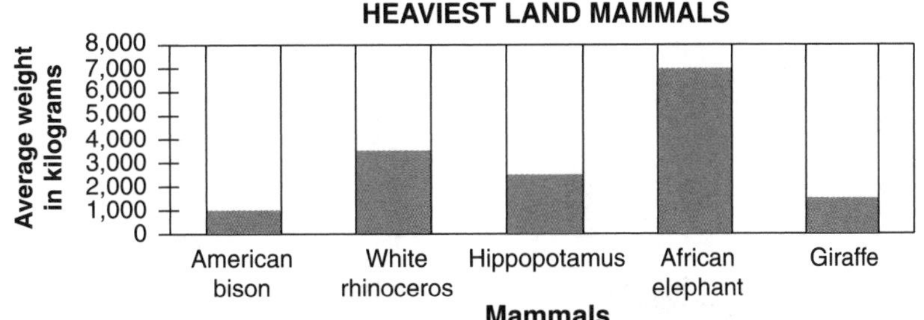

1. Which animal is the heaviest? What is its average weight?

Answer ______________________

2. Which animal is the lightest? What is its average weight?

Answer ______________________

3. How much more does a white rhinoceros weigh than a giraffe weighs?

Answer ______________________

4. A polar bear can weigh 400 kilograms less than the average American bison. How much can a polar bear weigh?

Answer ______________________

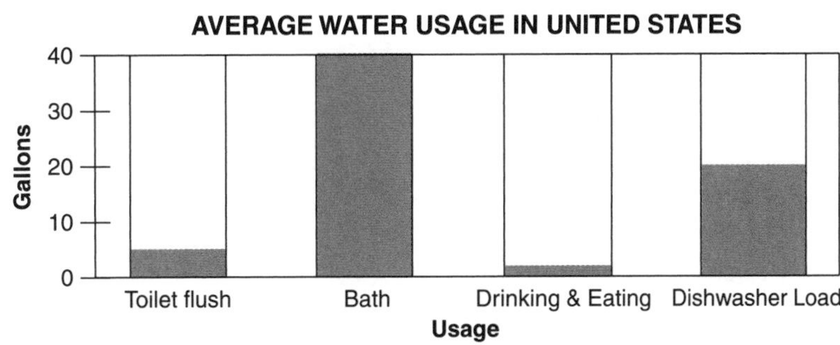

5. Which activity uses the least amount of water? How much water does it use?

Answer ______________________

6. Which activity uses the greatest amount of water? How much water does it use?

Answer ______________________

7. How much water would 3 dishwasher loads use?

Answer ______________________

8. How much water would you use if you took a bath every day for a week?

Answer ______________________

UNIT 6 Review

Write the time shown on each clock.

1.

a	b	c	d

______	______	______	______

Change the units of time.

2. 5 weeks = ________ days

3. 36 months = ________ years

4. 7 hours = ________ minutes

5. 3 days = ________ hours

Find when each event started or ended.

6. **Start:** 4:25 **Elapsed Time:** 2 hr 30 min

____

7. **End:** 11:00 **Elapsed Time:** 1 hr 45 min

____

Write each money amount using digits.

	a	b
8.	twenty-five dollars and six cents ______	nine dollars and fifteen cents ______
9.	five dollars and ten cents ______	eighty-nine cents ______

Find each answer.

	a	b	c	d
10.	$13.48 + 5.27	$27.63 − 24.79	$2.35 × 32	4)$4.96

Compare. Write <, >, or =.

	a	b
11.	36 in. ________ 2 ft.	5,000 g ________ 5 kg
12.	4 lb. ________ 32 oz.	400 cm ________ 3 m

Change the units of measure.

	a	*b*
13.	3 lb. = ________ oz.	4 T. = ________ lb.
14.	21 ft. = ________ yd.	2 mi. = ________ ft.
15.	8 c. = ________ pt.	10 pt. = ________ qt.
16.	2 L = ________ mL	700 cm = ________ m

Work backwards to solve each problem.

17. Charlie has $11.50 left after paying for his art supplies. He bought a canvas for $38.99 and paintbrushes for $42.70. Then he spent $85.00 on paints. How much money did he start with?

Answer ________________

18. Anita has to be at work by 8:30. She needs 45 minutes to get dressed and have breakfast. It takes her 25 minutes to drive to work. What time should she wake up in the morning?

Answer ________________

Use the graph to solve each problem.

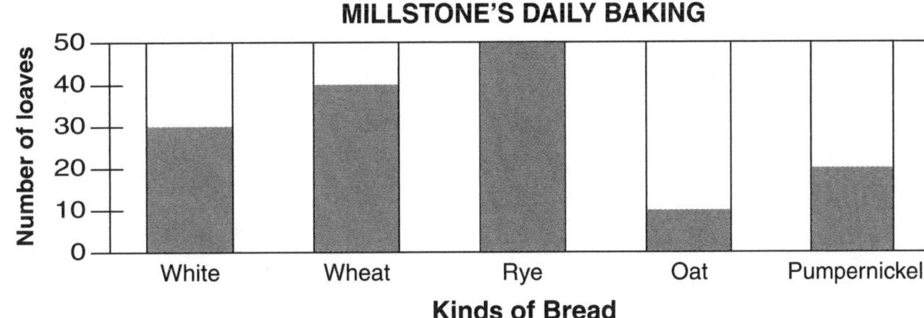

19. Which kind of bread does Millstone bake the greatest number of each day? How many loaves?

Answer ________________

20. How many more loaves of white bread than oat bread does Millstone bake?

Answer ________________

Unit 7
Fractions and Geometry

Meaning of Fractions

A **fraction** names a part of a whole. This circle has 4 equal parts. The purple part is $\frac{1}{4}$ of the circle.

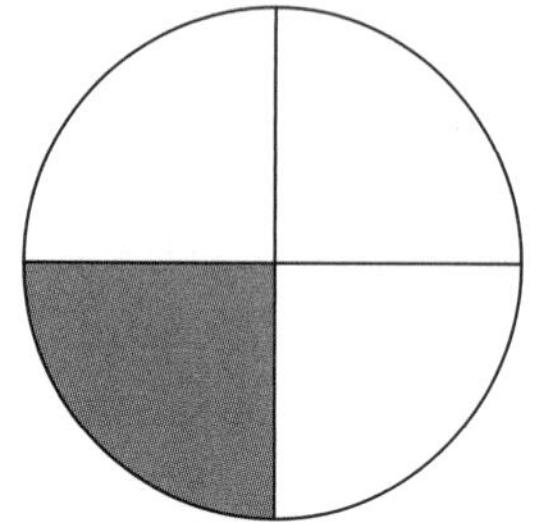

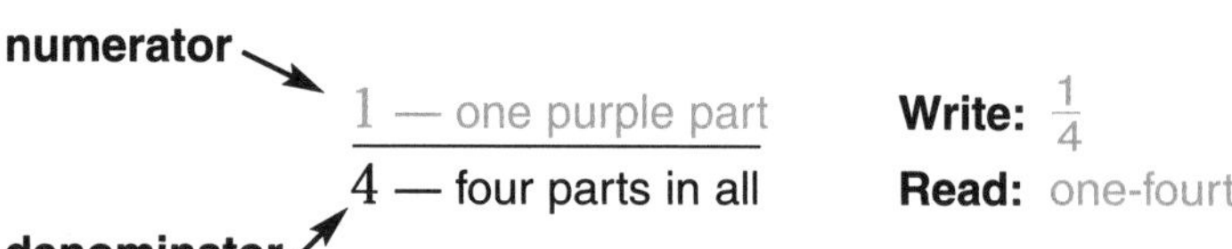

Use the pictures to complete Exercises 1–6.

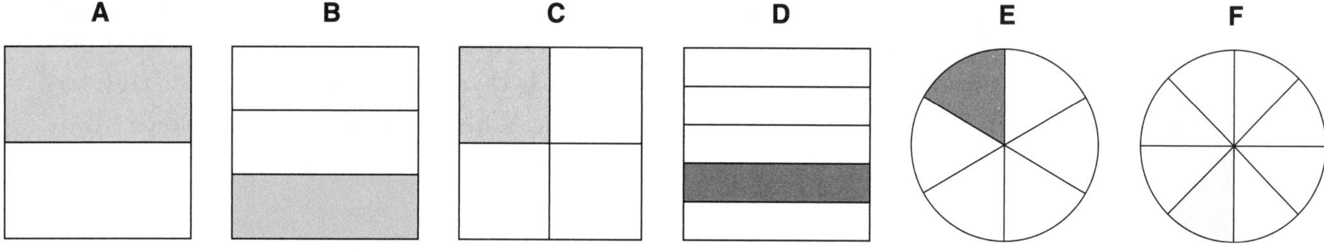

1. Square A has how many equal parts? ___2___

   The green part is ___$\frac{1}{2}$___ or ___one-half___ of the square.

2. Square B has how many equal parts? ________

   The orange part is ________ or ________________ of the square.

3. Square C has how many equal parts? ________

   The blue part is ________ or ________________ of the square.

4. Square D has how many equal parts? ________

   The purple part is ________ or ________________ of the square.

5. Circle E has how many equal parts? ________

   The pink part is ________ or ________________ of the circle.

6. Circle F has how many equal parts? ________

   The yellow part is ________ or ________________ of the circle.

Using Fractions

A fraction can name part of a group. Four of the eight cookies are chocolate chip. Or, four-eighths of the cookies are chocolate chip.

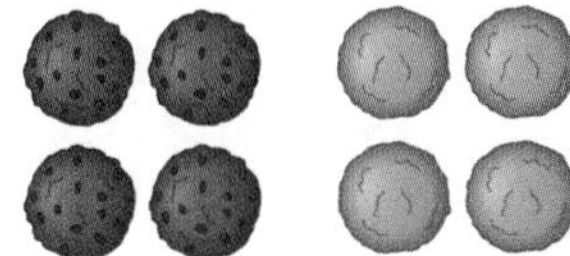

$\frac{4}{8}$ of the cookies are chocolate chip.

You can use fractions to find part of a group. To find $\frac{1}{2}$ of 8, divide 8 by 2.

$8 \div 2 = 4$

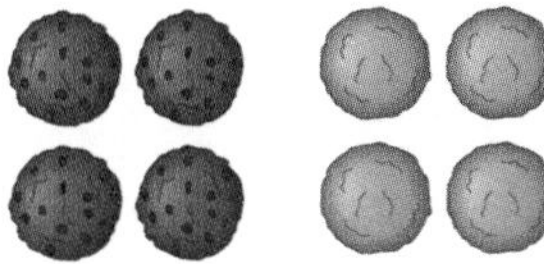

$\frac{1}{2}$ of 8, or 4, of the cookies are chocolate chip.

Find: $\frac{1}{2}$ of 20

To find $\frac{1}{2}$, divide by 2.

$20 \div 2 = 10$

$\frac{1}{2}$ of 20 = 10

Find: one-fourth of 16

To find $\frac{1}{4}$, divide by 4.

$16 \div 4 = 8$

$\frac{1}{4}$ of 16 = 4

Find each number.

	a	b
1.	To find $\frac{1}{3}$, divide by ___3___.	To find one-sixth, divide by ______.
2.	To find $\frac{1}{8}$, divide by ______.	To find one-tenth, divide by ______.
3.	$\frac{1}{4}$ of 20 = ______	One-third of 18 is ______.
4.	$\frac{1}{2}$ of 50 = ______	One-sixth of 42 is ______.
5.	$\frac{1}{3}$ of 18 = ______	One-half of $1.00 is ______.
6.	$\frac{1}{10}$ of $20.00 = ______	One-eighth of $64.00 is ______.
7.	$\frac{1}{6}$ of $12.00 = ______	One-fifth of 25 is ______.

Adding Fractions

Like fractions are fractions with the same denominators. To add like fractions, add only the numerators. Then use the same denominator for the sum.

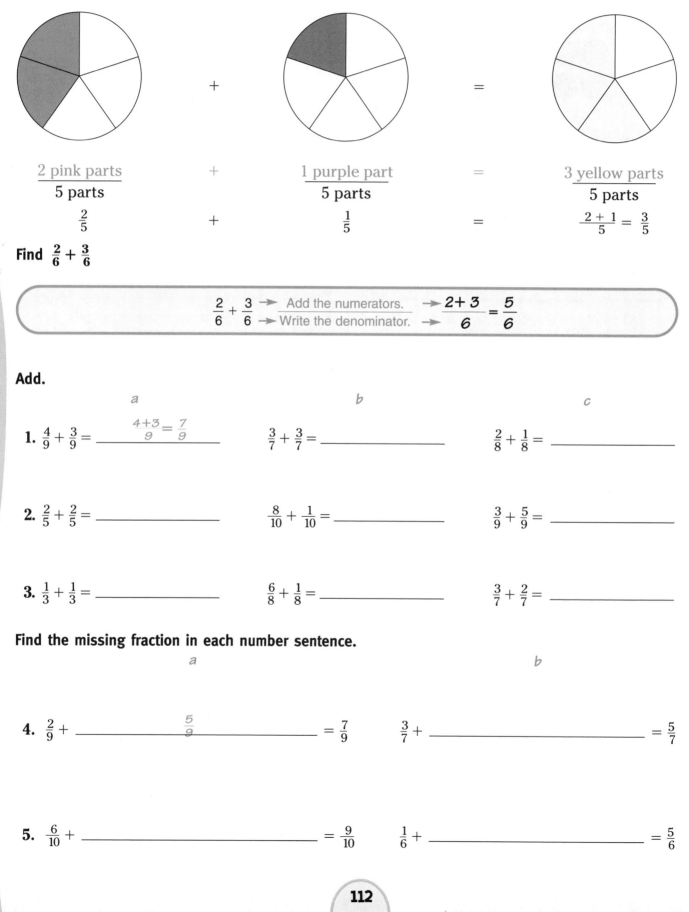

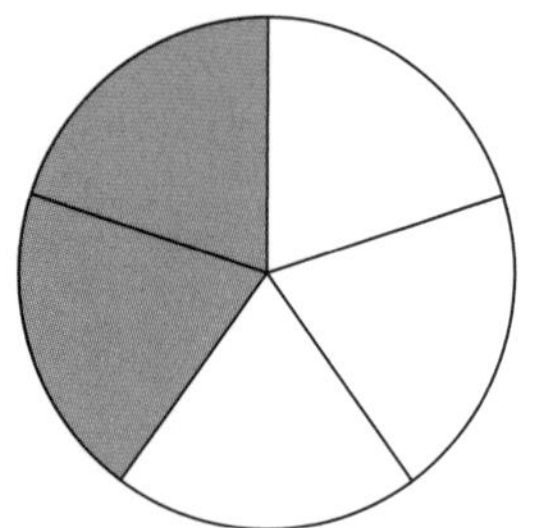 + 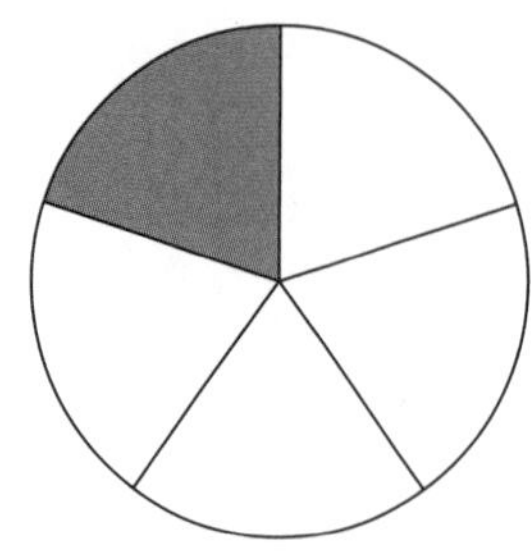 = 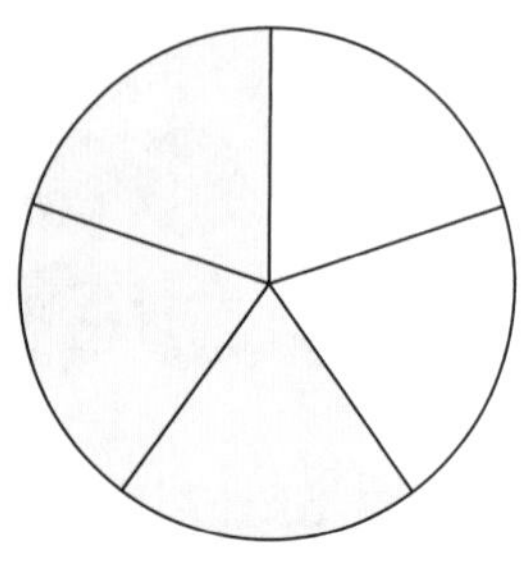

$\frac{\text{2 pink parts}}{\text{5 parts}}$	+	$\frac{\text{1 purple part}}{\text{5 parts}}$	=	$\frac{\text{3 yellow parts}}{\text{5 parts}}$
$\frac{2}{5}$	+	$\frac{1}{5}$	=	$\frac{2+1}{5} = \frac{3}{5}$

Find $\frac{2}{6} + \frac{3}{6}$

$\frac{2}{6} + \frac{3}{6}$ → Add the numerators. / Write the denominator. → $\frac{2+3}{6} = \frac{5}{6}$

Add.

	a	b	c
1.	$\frac{4}{9} + \frac{3}{9} =$ $\frac{4+3}{9} = \frac{7}{9}$	$\frac{3}{7} + \frac{3}{7} =$ ______	$\frac{2}{8} + \frac{1}{8} =$ ______
2.	$\frac{2}{5} + \frac{2}{5} =$ ______	$\frac{8}{10} + \frac{1}{10} =$ ______	$\frac{3}{9} + \frac{5}{9} =$ ______
3.	$\frac{1}{3} + \frac{1}{3} =$ ______	$\frac{6}{8} + \frac{1}{8} =$ ______	$\frac{3}{7} + \frac{2}{7} =$ ______

Find the missing fraction in each number sentence.

	a	b
4.	$\frac{2}{9} +$ $\frac{5}{9}$ $= \frac{7}{9}$	$\frac{3}{7} +$ ______ $= \frac{5}{7}$
5.	$\frac{6}{10} +$ ______ $= \frac{9}{10}$	$\frac{1}{6} +$ ______ $= \frac{5}{6}$

Subtracting Fractions

To subtract like fractions, subtract only the numerators. Then use the same denominator for the difference.

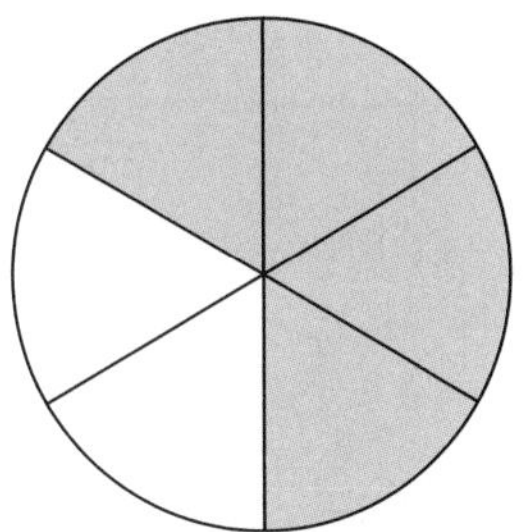

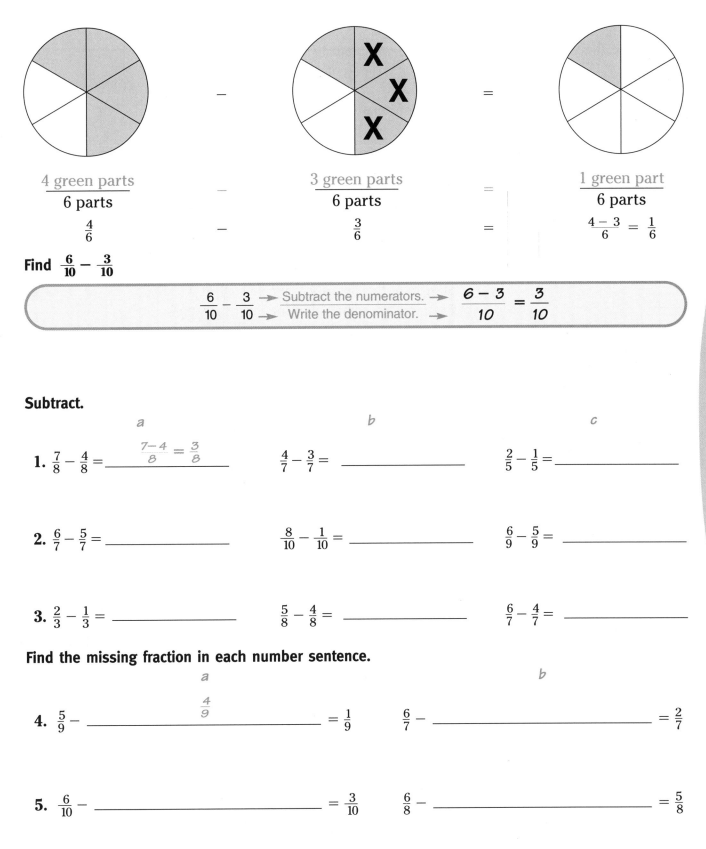

4 green parts / 6 parts	−	3 green parts / 6 parts	=	1 green part / 6 parts
$\frac{4}{6}$	−	$\frac{3}{6}$	=	$\frac{4-3}{6} = \frac{1}{6}$

Find $\frac{6}{10} - \frac{3}{10}$

$\frac{6}{10} - \frac{3}{10}$ → Subtract the numerators. → Write the denominator. → $\frac{6-3}{10} = \frac{3}{10}$

Subtract.

	a	b	c
1.	$\frac{7}{8} - \frac{4}{8} = \frac{7-4}{8} = \frac{3}{8}$	$\frac{4}{7} - \frac{3}{7} =$ ______	$\frac{2}{5} - \frac{1}{5} =$ ______
2.	$\frac{6}{7} - \frac{5}{7} =$ ______	$\frac{8}{10} - \frac{1}{10} =$ ______	$\frac{6}{9} - \frac{5}{9} =$ ______
3.	$\frac{2}{3} - \frac{1}{3} =$ ______	$\frac{5}{8} - \frac{4}{8} =$ ______	$\frac{6}{7} - \frac{4}{7} =$ ______

Find the missing fraction in each number sentence.

	a	b
4.	$\frac{5}{9} -$ $\frac{4}{9}$ $= \frac{1}{9}$	$\frac{6}{7} -$ ______ $= \frac{2}{7}$
5.	$\frac{6}{10} -$ ______ $= \frac{3}{10}$	$\frac{6}{8} -$ ______ $= \frac{5}{8}$

Problem-Solving Method: Make an Organized List

Acme Hardware Store sells three sizes of screws: $\frac{1}{4}$ inch, $\frac{1}{2}$ inch, and $\frac{3}{4}$ inch. All of the screws come in two styles: Phillips head or flat head. How many different kinds of screws does the store sell?

Understand the problem.

- **What do you want to know?**
  how many different kinds of screws they sell

- **What information is given?**
  Sizes: $\frac{1}{4}$ inch, $\frac{1}{2}$ inch, and $\frac{3}{4}$ inch
  Styles: Phillips head or flat head

Plan how to solve it.

- **What method can you use?**
  You can make a list of the different style-size combinations. Then count the combinations.

- **How can you use this method to solve the problem?**
  Start with the first style and list all of its sizes.
  Then do the same thing for the other style.

Style	Size
Phillips head	$\frac{1}{4}$ inch
Phillips head	$\frac{1}{2}$ inch
Phillips head	$\frac{3}{4}$ inch

Style	Size
flat head	$\frac{1}{4}$ inch
flat head	$\frac{1}{2}$ inch
flat head	$\frac{3}{4}$ inch

Solve it.

- **What is the answer?**
  Acme Hardware Store sells 6 different kinds of screws.

Look back and check your answer.

- **Is your answer reasonable?**

You can check by making a tree diagram.

The counts match. The answer is reasonable.

Style	Size	Combination
Phillips head →	$\frac{1}{4}$ inch	$\frac{1}{4}$-inch Phillips head
	$\frac{1}{2}$ inch	$\frac{1}{2}$-inch Phillips head
	$\frac{3}{4}$ inch	$\frac{3}{4}$-inch Phillips head
flat head →	$\frac{1}{4}$ inch	$\frac{1}{4}$-inch flat head
	$\frac{1}{2}$ inch	$\frac{1}{2}$-inch flat head
	$\frac{3}{4}$ inch	$\frac{3}{4}$-inch flat head

Make an organized list to solve each problem.

1. *City Paper* runs color and black-and-white advertisements. The ads can fill $\frac{1}{2}$, $\frac{1}{4}$, or $\frac{3}{4}$ of a page. Mario's Pizza wants to place an ad. How many different choices do they have?

Answer ______________________

2. Pop's Ice Cream Shop lets you choose 1 sauce and 1 topping for your sundae. They have hot fudge and caramel syrup. The two toppings are nuts or sprinkles. How many different sundaes can you choose from?

Answer ______________________

3. Ken has $0.60 in U.S. coins. He only has 1 quarter and no half-dollars or pennies. What are all the possible coin combinations Ken could have?

Answer ______________________

____

____

____

Plotting Points on a Coordinate Grid

A **point** is an exact location in space. A **coordinate grid** is a graph with horizontal and vertical lines. To **plot**, or locate, a point, use an ordered pair. An **ordered pair** is two numbers that give directions to a point.

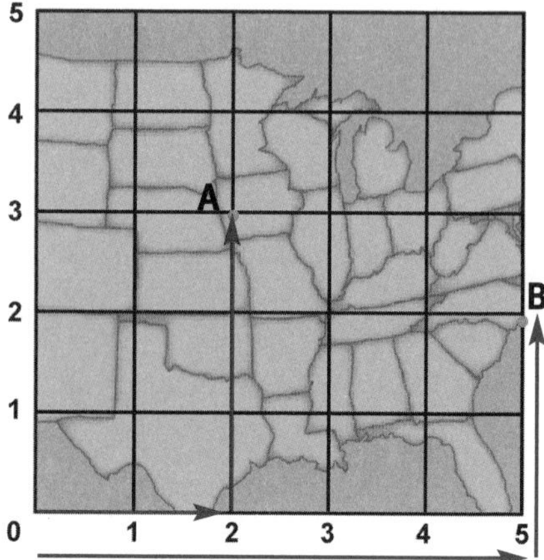

Plot point (2,3).

1. Start at 0.
2. Move 2 spaces to the right.
3. Move 3 spaces up.
4. Label your point with a capital letter, *A*.

Name the ordered pair for Point B.

1. Start at 0.
2. Count how many spaces to the right. (5)
3. Count how many spaces up. (2)
4. Write the numbers as an ordered pair. (5,2)

Plot each point on the coordinate grid.

	a	b
1.	point *A* (4,3)	point *B* (1,1)
2.	point *C* (3,6)	point *D* (6,7)
3.	point *E* (8,0)	point *F* (8,4)
4.	point *G* (9,2)	point *H* (2,8)

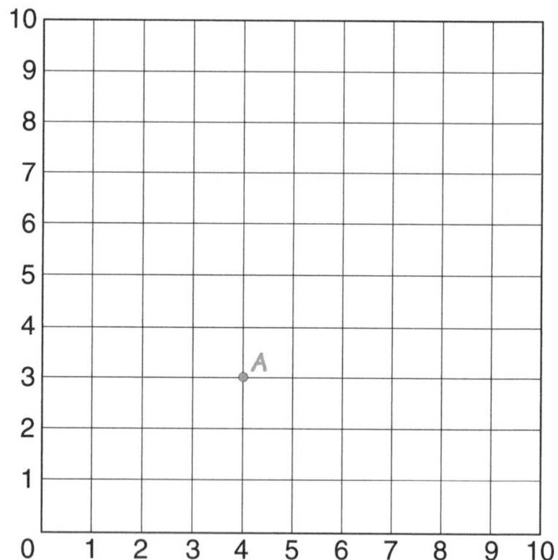

Name the ordered pair for each point.

5. point *L* (2,7)

6. point *M* ____________

7. point *N* ____________

8. point *O* ____________

9. point *P* ____________

10. point *Q* ____________

11. point *R* ____________

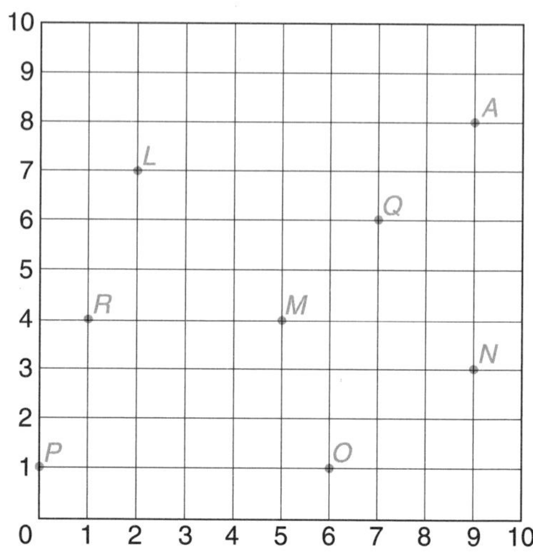

Lines, Rays, and Line Segments

A **line** is an endless straight path.

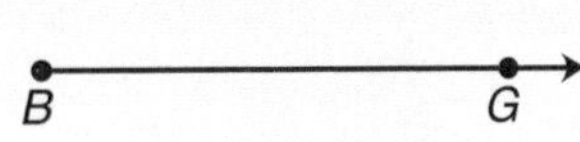

Say: line *AB* or line *BA*
Write: $\overleftrightarrow{AB}$ or $\overleftrightarrow{BA}$

A **line segment** is a straight path between two points.

R S

Say: line segment *RS* or line segment *SR*
Write: $\overline{RS}$ or $\overline{SR}$

A **ray** is an endless straight path starting at one point.

B G

Say: ray *BG*
Write: $\overrightarrow{BG}$

Name each figure. Write *line*, *line segment*, or *ray*.

a b c d

1.

line segment ______ ______ ______ ______

Name each figure using symbols.

a b c d

2.

$\overline{PQ}$ or $\overline{QP}$ ______ ______ ______

Use the drawing at right for Exercises 3–6.

3. Name a ray. $\overrightarrow{PB}$ or ray PB

4. Name a line. ______

5. Name a line segment. ______

6. Name a point. ______

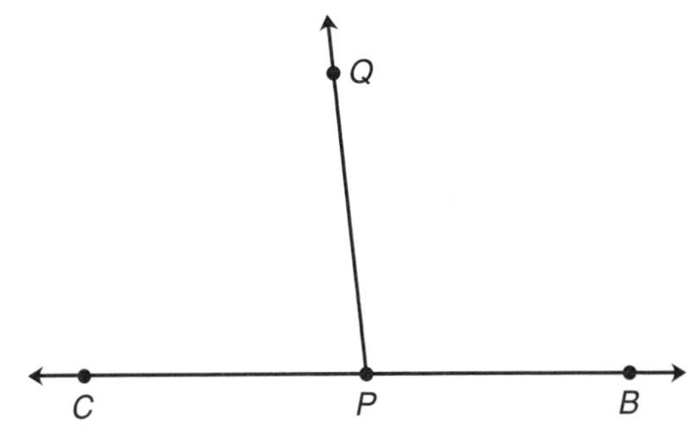

Exploring Angles

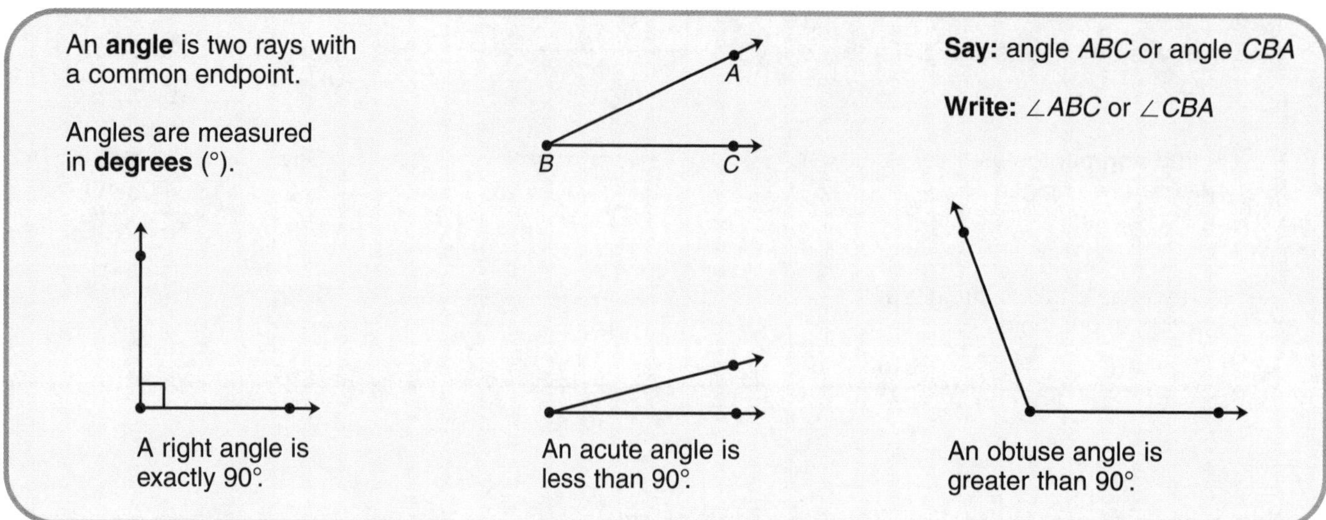

An **angle** is two rays with a common endpoint.

Angles are measured in **degrees** (°).

Say: angle *ABC* or angle *CBA*

Write: ∠*ABC* or ∠*CBA*

A right angle is exactly 90°.

An acute angle is less than 90°.

An obtuse angle is greater than 90°.

Name each angle using symbols.

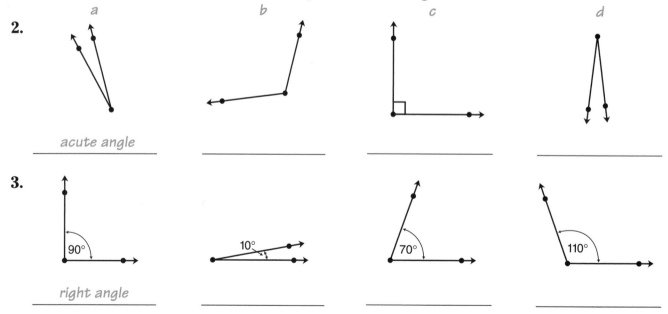

1.

a

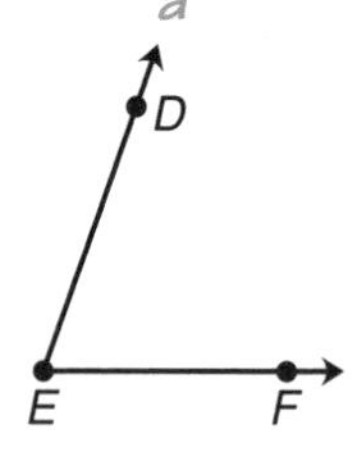

∠ DEF or ∠ FED

b

Q
S
R

c

L
M
N

d

G
E
F

Name each angle. Write *right angle*, *acute angle*, or *obtuse angle*.

2.

a

acute angle

b

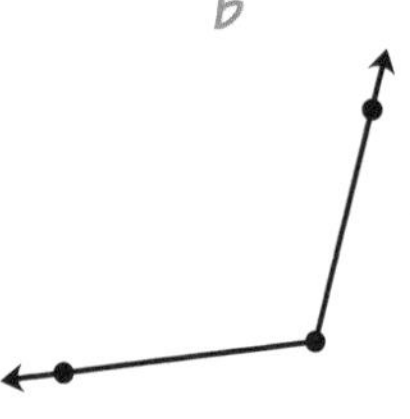

c

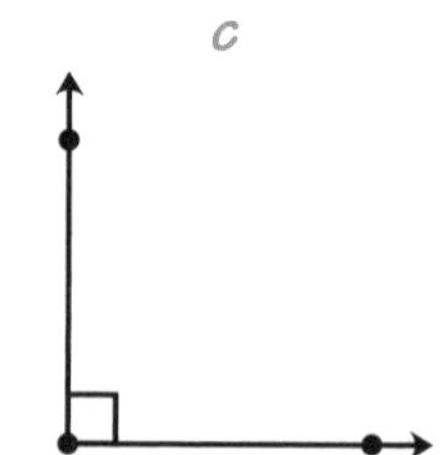

d

3.

a

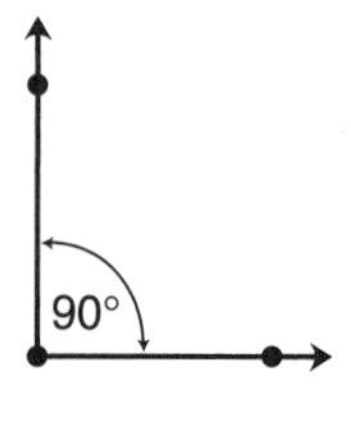

right angle

b

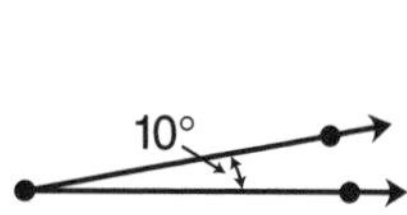

c

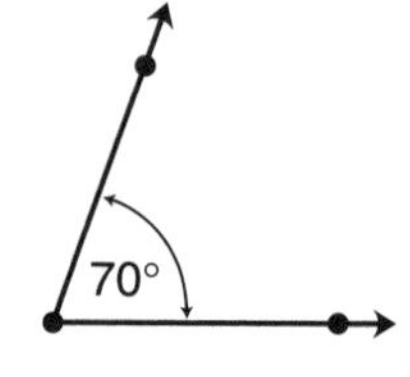

d

110°

Perimeter

Perimeter is the distance around a figure.

To find the perimeter of a figure, add the lengths of its sides.

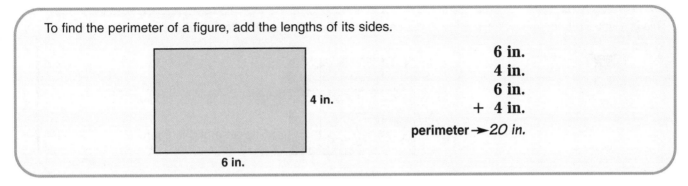

4 in.

6 in.

$$\begin{array}{r} \textbf{6 in.} \\ \textbf{4 in.} \\ \textbf{6 in.} \\ + \ \textbf{4 in.} \\ \hline \end{array}$$

perimeter → *20 in.*

Find the perimeter of each figure.

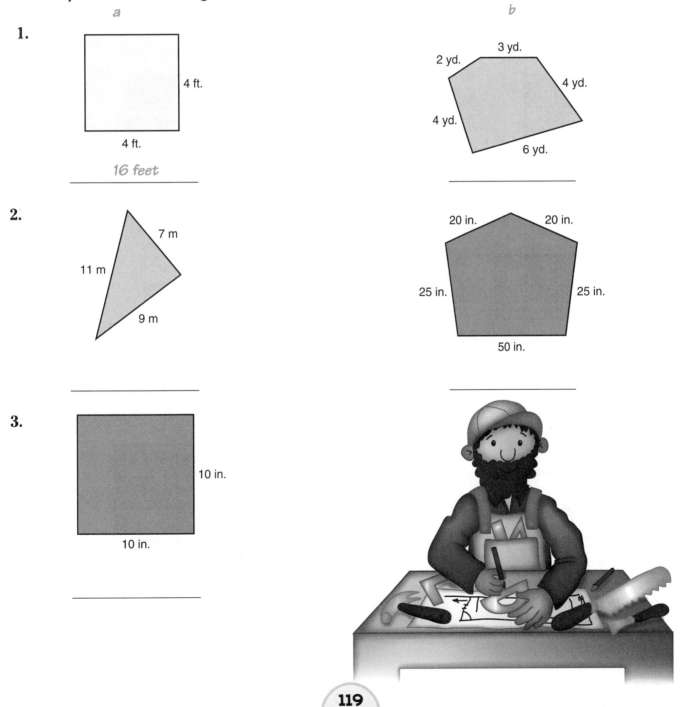

a | *b*

1.

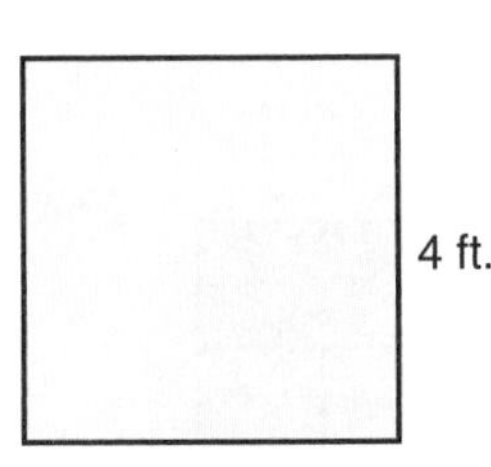

16 feet

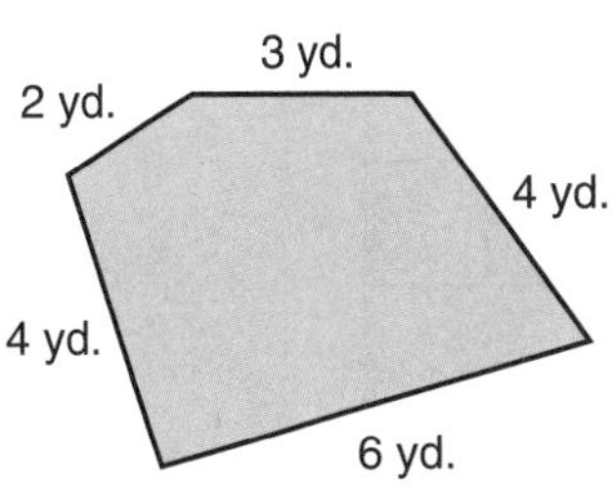

____

2.

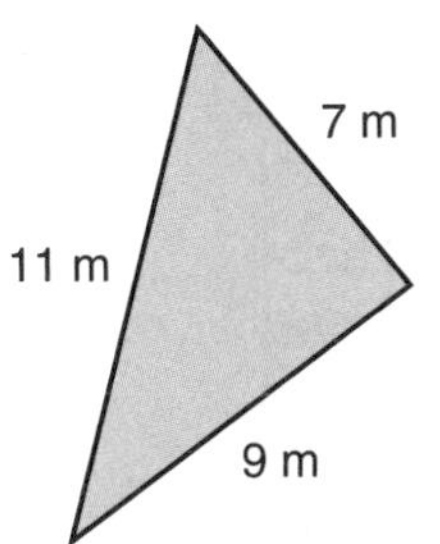

____

20 in.
20 in.
25 in.
25 in.
50 in.

____

3.

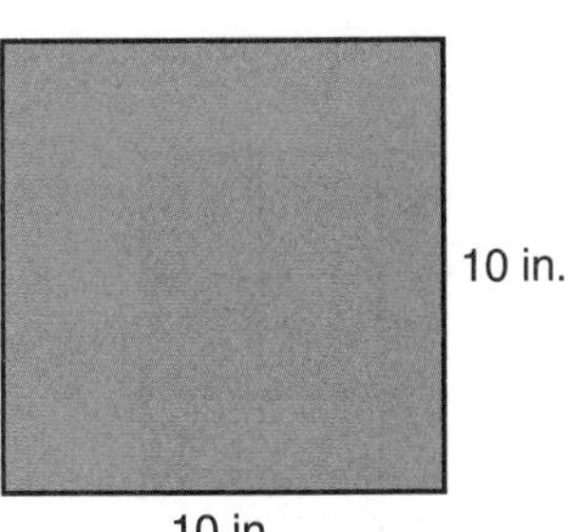

____

Area

The **area** of a figure is the number of **square units** that cover its surface.

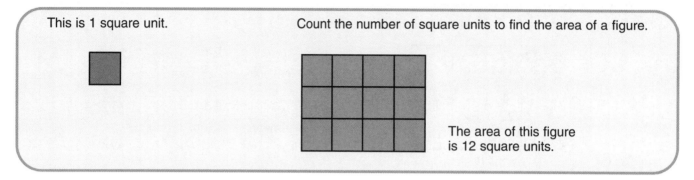

This is 1 square unit.

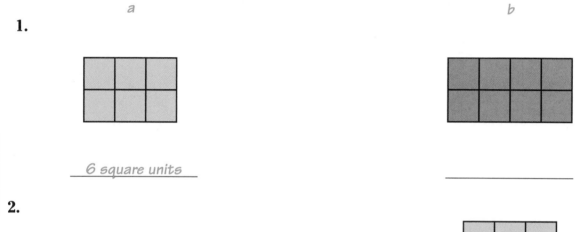

Count the number of square units to find the area of a figure.

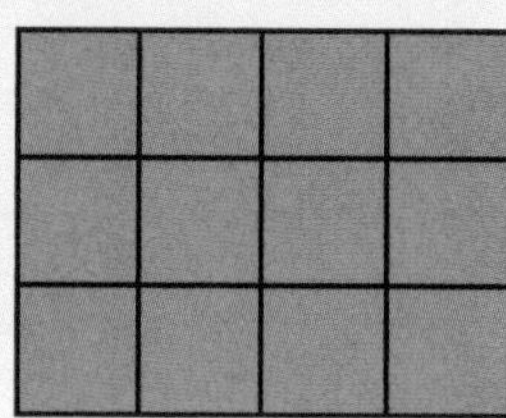

The area of this figure is 12 square units.

Find the area of each figure.

a b

1.

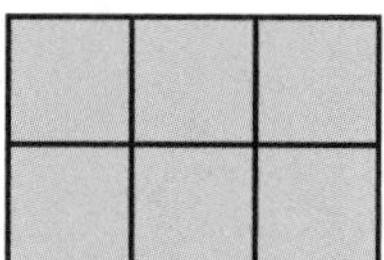

6 square units

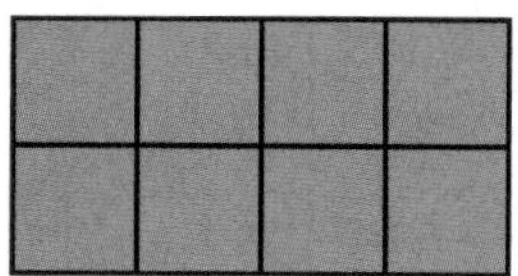

____

2.

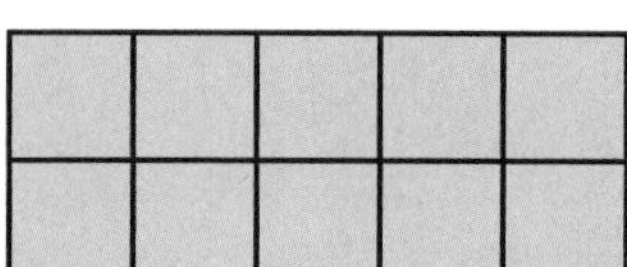

____

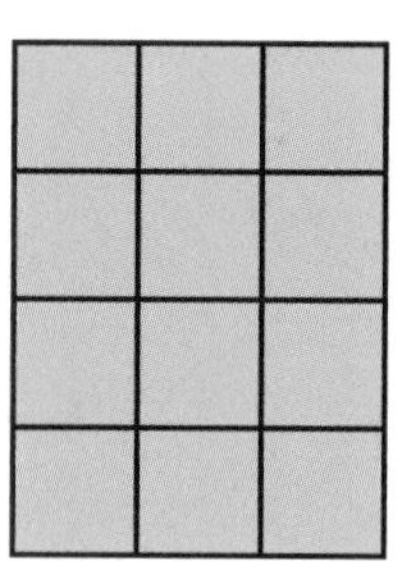

____

3.

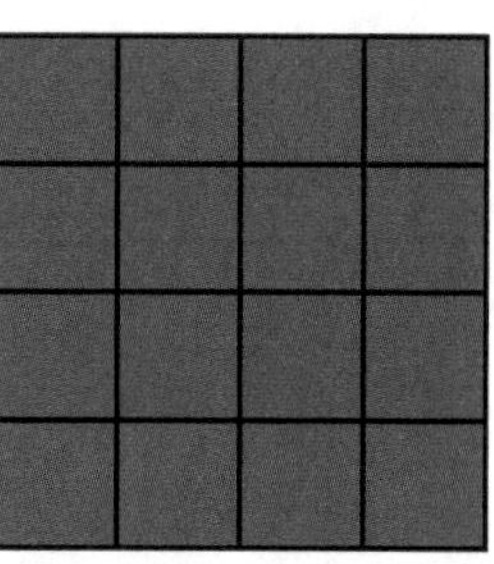

____

____

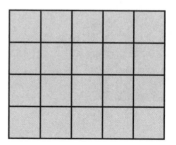

Problem-Solving Method: Use a Formula

Colleen painted a picture that is 6 feet long and 6 feet wide. How much wood will she need to make a frame?

Understand the problem.

- **What do you want to know?**
  how much wood she needs to make a frame
- **What information is given?**
  The picture is 6 feet long and 6 feet wide.

Plan how to solve it.

- **What method can you use?**
  You can use a formula. Since she wants to know the distance around a figure, she needs a formula for perimeter.

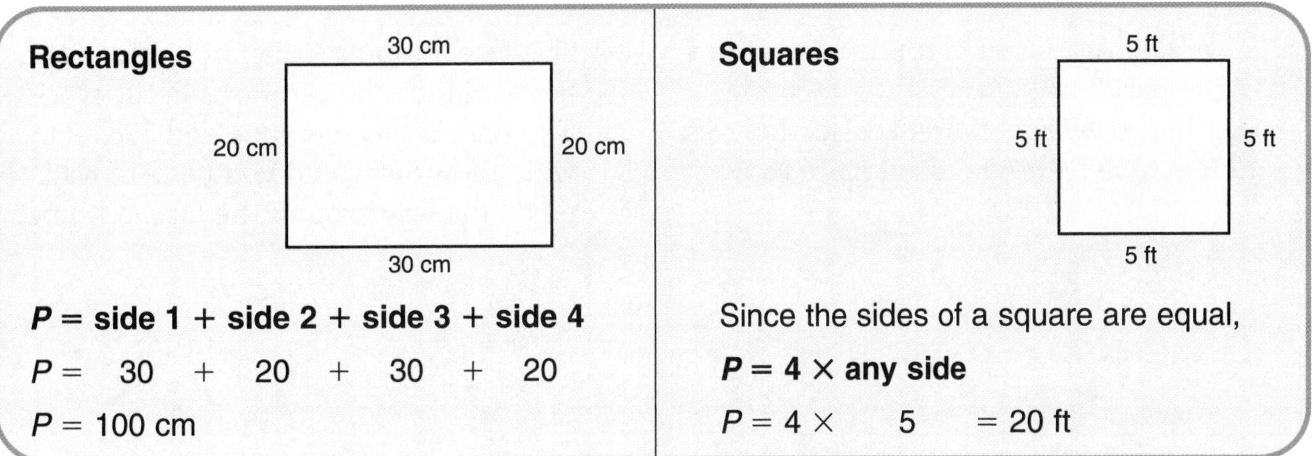

Rectangles
30 cm
20 cm
20 cm
30 cm
P = side 1 + side 2 + side 3 + side 4
P = 30 + 20 + 30 + 20
P = 100 cm
Squares
5 ft
5 ft
5 ft
5 ft
Since the sides of a square are equal,
P = 4 × any side
P = 4 × 5 = 20 ft

Solve it.

- **How can you use this method to solve the problem?**
  Since Colleen's picture is a square, she can use the formula for the perimeter of a square.

P = 4 × any side
P = 4 × 6
P = 24 feet

- **What is the answer?**
  Colleen needs 24 feet of wood to make the frame.

Look back and check your answer.

- **Is your answer reasonable?**
  You can check by adding the side lengths.
  The sum matches the answer from the formula.
  The answer is reasonable.

$$\begin{array}{r} 6 \text{ ft} \\ 6 \text{ ft} \\ 6 \text{ ft} \\ +\ 6 \text{ ft} \\ \hline 24 \text{ ft} \end{array}$$

Use a formula to solve each problem.

1. An NBA basketball court is 94 feet long and 50 feet wide. What is the perimeter of the court?

Answer ______________________

2. Little League baseball diamonds have 60 feet between bases. How far does a player run when she hits a home run?

Answer ______________________

3. Steve and Aretha each roped-off sections of the park for picnics. Steve's section was 10 feet by 8 feet. Aretha's section was 12 feet by 5 feet. Who used more rope?

Answer ______________________

4. The Ocean Dome in Japan is one of the largest indoor water parks in the world. The park is 985 feet long and 328 feet wide. How far would you have to walk to go all the way around the Ocean Dome?

Answer ______________________

5. Raul's vegetable garden measures 15 feet in length and 12 feet in width. How much fencing will he need to surround the garden?

Answer ______________________

Find each number.

	a	b	c
1.	$\frac{1}{5}$ of 20 = ______	$\frac{1}{4}$ of 16 = ______	$\frac{1}{3}$ of 9 = ______
2.	$\frac{1}{2}$ of 36 = ______	$\frac{1}{6}$ of 18 = ______	$\frac{1}{7}$ of 21 = ______

Add.

	a	b	c
3.	$\frac{3}{8} + \frac{4}{8} =$ ______	$\frac{3}{11} + \frac{7}{11} =$ ______	$\frac{1}{4} + \frac{2}{4} =$ ______
4.	$\frac{3}{5} + \frac{1}{5} =$ ______	$\frac{2}{9} + \frac{3}{9} =$ ______	$\frac{4}{8} + \frac{3}{8} =$ ______

Subtract.

	a	b	c
5.	$\frac{3}{4} - \frac{2}{4} =$ ______	$\frac{5}{11} - \frac{3}{11} =$ ______	$\frac{5}{7} - \frac{2}{7} =$ ______
6.	$\frac{8}{9} - \frac{4}{9} =$ ______	$\frac{6}{7} - \frac{2}{7} =$ ______	$\frac{4}{5} - \frac{3}{5} =$ ______

Plot each point on the coordinate grid.

7. point A (1,3)

8. point B (0,5)

9. point C (2,0)

10. point D (7,5)

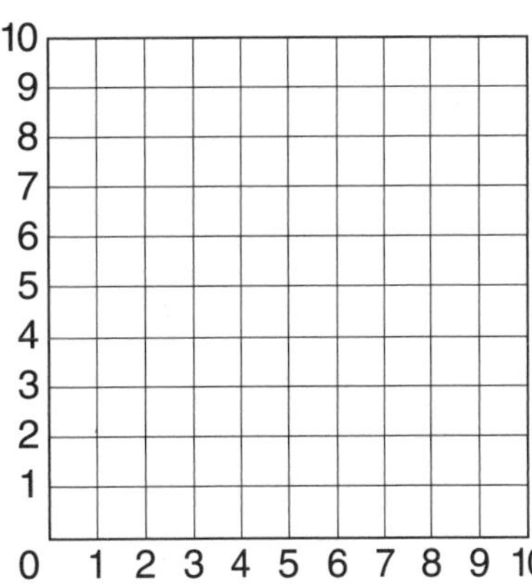

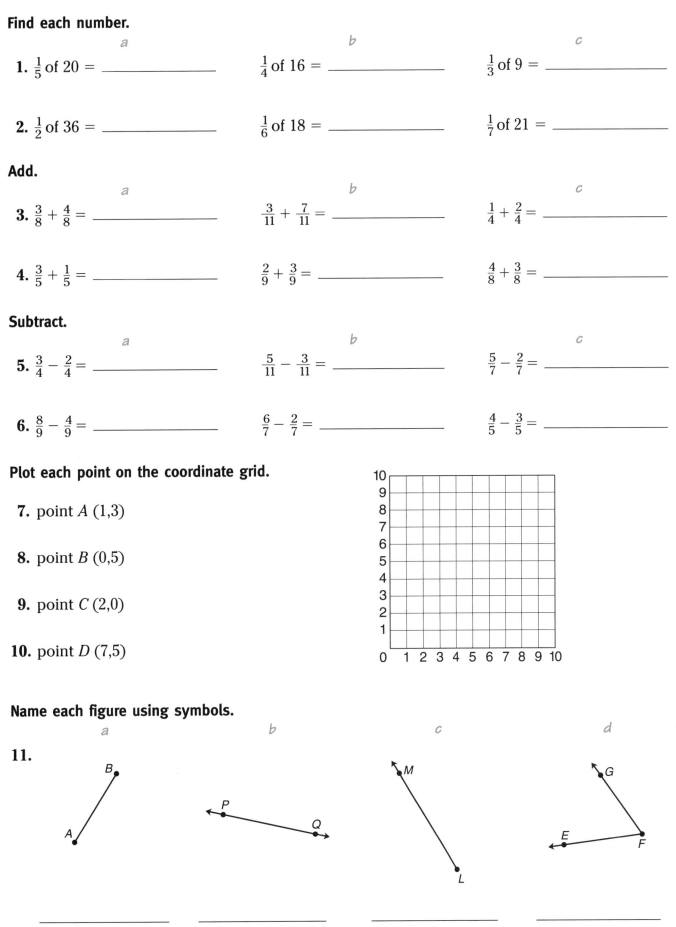

Name each figure using symbols.

11.

a

B
A

b

P
Q

c

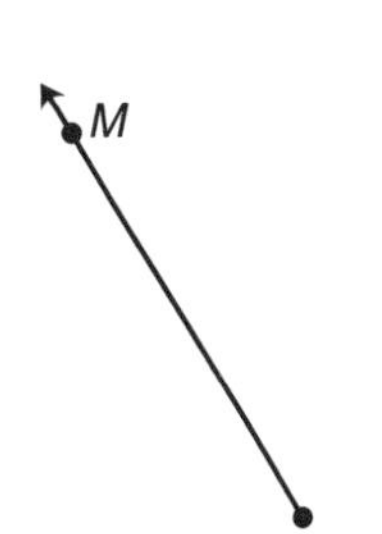

d

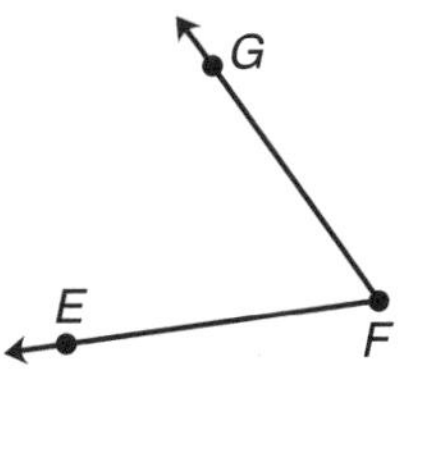

______ ______ ______ ______

Name each angle. Write *right angle, acute angle,* or *obtuse angle.*

12.

a

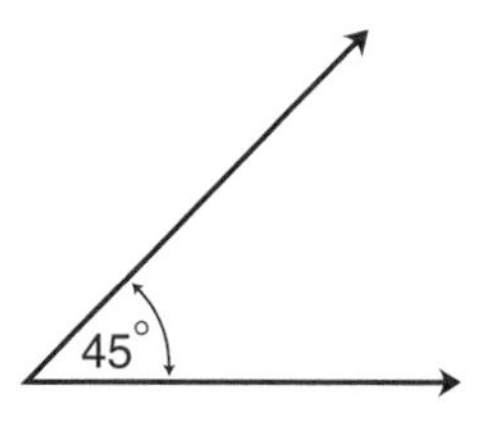

____

b

190°

____

c

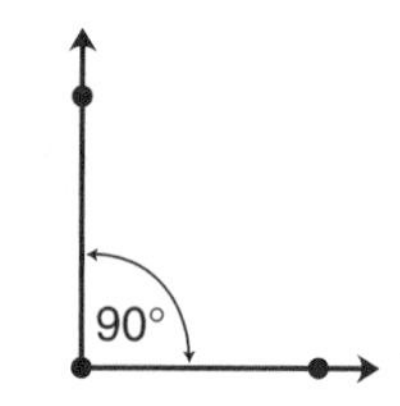

____

d

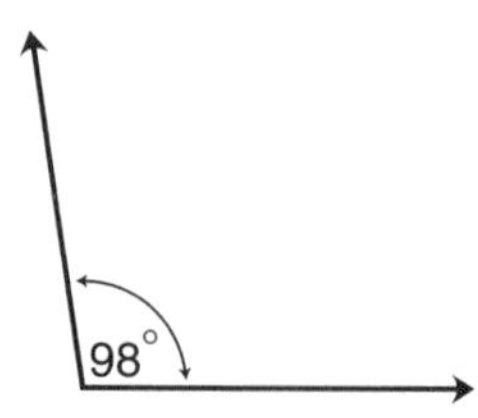

____

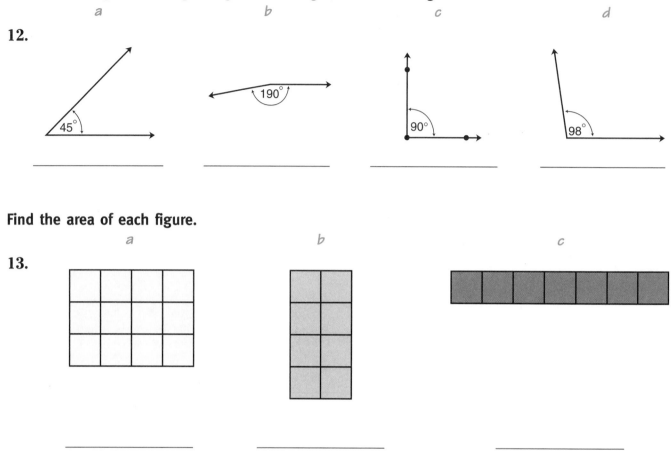

Find the area of each figure.

13.

a

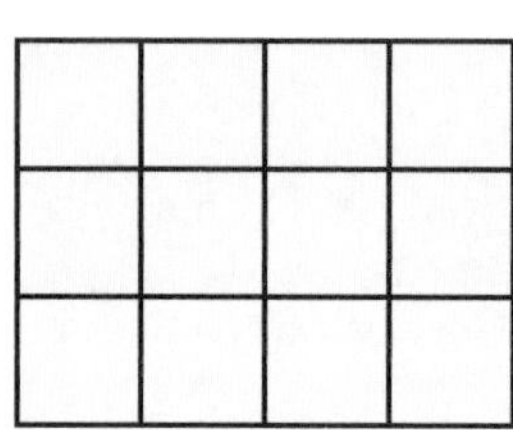

____

b

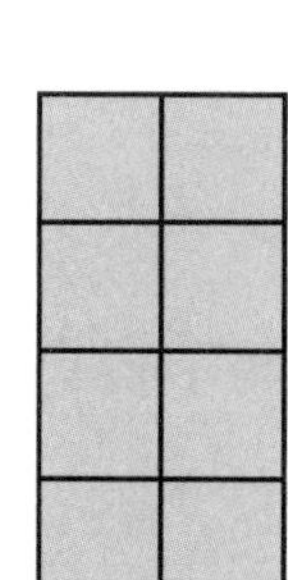

____

c

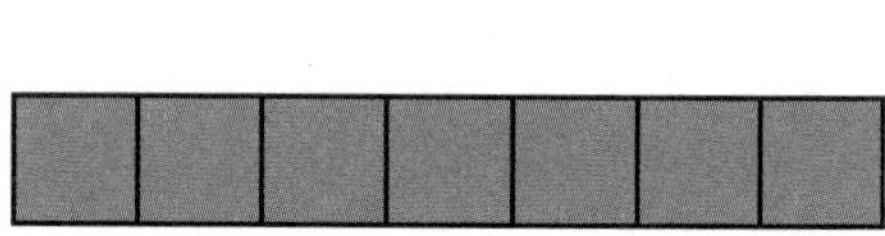

____

Use a formula to solve each problem.

14. A photograph is 8 inches wide by 10 inches long. How much wood is needed to frame the photo?

Answer ______________________

15. One side of John's square pool measures 10 meters. What is the perimeter of the pool?

Answer ______________________

Make an organized list to solve each problem.

16. The cafeteria serves chicken, tuna, and ham sandwiches. They have white, rye, and wheat bread. How many different sandwich choices do they serve?

Answer ______________________

17. Gina packed 1 pair of jeans and 1 pair of shorts for the weekend. She also brought 3 shirts: blue, white, and green. How many different outfits can she wear?

Answer ______________________

Answer Key

Page 6

	a	b	c
1.	2,561	4,739	6,268
2.	8,091	5,473	3,502
3.	6,648	9,722	2,059
4.	3,541	1,943	5,540
5.	7,452		
6.	3,095		
7.	8,620		
8.	600	6,000	4
9.	30	300	900
10.	8,000	6,000	4

Page 7

1.						2,	3	9	5
2.				4	1	8,	7	0	2
3.		2	0,	0	9	1,	5	7	6
4.							9	8	7
5.					1	3,	8	2	0
6.			5,	4	8	2,	6	3	7

	a	b
7.	tens	ten thousands
8.	millions	hundreds
9.	ones	ten millions
10.	thousands	hundred thousands
11.	7 hundreds or 700	2 hundred millions or 200,000,000
12.	0 ones or 0	4 hundred thousands or 400,000
13.	3 millions or 3,000,000	9 ten millions or 90,000,000
14.	5 tens or 50	0 thousands or 0

Page 8

	a	b	c
1.	345,156	10,105	221,689
2.	2,970,534	369,571	50,148
3.	17,652,017	5,304,602	189,360
4.	529,031		
5.	76,411		
6.	8,050,200		
7.	2,307		
8.	94,655		

9. twenty-three thousand, eight hundred eighty
10. seven hundred thirty thousand, six hundred four
11. nineteen thousand, forty-two
12. five million, two hundred eight thousand

Page 9

	a	b	c
1.	>	<	<
2.	<	>	>
3.	<	=	>
4.	>	>	<
5.	=	<	>
6.	>	>	<

Page 11

1. Great white: 32,000 lb.
2. Chamberlain: 31,419 pt.; Jordan: 29,277 pt.; Abdul-Jabbar: 38,387 pt.
3. "Beast": 7,400 ft.; "Shivering Timbers": 5,384 ft.; "Mean Streak": 5,427 ft.

Page 12

1. eighty-eight thousand, eight hundred forty
2. two hundred fifty million
3. 9,365
4. 45,180
5. 661
6. 4,145
7. two thousand, five hundred fifty-five
8. fifty-five thousand, seventy

Page 13

	a	b	c	d
1.	12	7	13	9
2.	9	10	10	11
3.	4	4	15	7
4.	10	4	13	6
5.	8	8	9	8
6.	16	3	11	15

	a	b	c	d	e	f
7.	10	10	7	9	17	14
8.	13	10	16	6	9	11
9.	7	12	11	12	14	5

Page 14

	a	b	c	d	e
1.	29	49	89	68	99
2.	57	95	89	90	89
3.	961	653	727	968	679
4.	158	879	754	290	559
5.	99	286	789		
6.	879	495	336		

Page 15

	a	b	c	d	e
1.	81	61	54	62	53
2.	122	124	122	132	133
3.	485	657	539	892	418
4.	1,423	1,120	1,310	1,323	1,190
5.	61	1,063	429		

Page 16

	a	b	c	d	e
1.	133	136	133	155	176
2.	1,510	526	769	1,018	1,304
3.	956	1,127	727	1,171	1,361
4.	806	849			

Page 17

	a	b	c	d	e	f
1.	7	4	5	7		
2.	2	9	8	3		
3.	9	6	0	5		
4.	3	6	5	0		
5.	7	6	9	3		
6.	8	1	7	7		
7.	4	6	6	8	1	6
8.	5	10	9	8	4	3
9.	6	7	9	1	5	6

Page 18

	a	b	c	d	e
1.	23	70	43	52	31
2.	17	14	40	21	35
3.	435	500	835	334	234
4.	349	541	154	223	434
5.	35	324	322		
6.	425	740	858		

Page 19

	a	b	c	d	e
1.	34	26	48	8	13
2.	33	19	23	77	39
3.	76	75	78	248	250
4.	378	732	326	480	189
5.	77	286	188		

Page 20

	a	b	c	d	e
1.	19	145	188	239	56
2.	358	478	387	77	544
3.	476	169	130	756	183
4.	276	187	158		

Page 21

	a	b	c	d	e
1.	813	474	893	788	416
2.	787	812	768	1,073	999
3.	240	251	234	7	222
4.	167	248	363	557	208
5.	1,075	1,262	152		

Page 22

	a	b	c	d
1.	520	740	260	450
2.	220	870	340	610
3.	880	730	930	860
4.	800	700	200	700
5.	300	500	300	500
6.	900	800	900	100
7.	2,000	4,000	5,000	9,000
8.	4,000	8,000	6,000	2,000
9.	8,000	2,000	2,000	5,000

Page 23

	a	b	c	d
1.	50	160	120	70
2.	90	100	80	170
3.	800	700	800	1,100
4.	700	1,400	1,500	500
5.	120	600	1,200	

Page 24

	a	b	c	d
1.	20	10	30	10
2.	10	70	40	70
3.	200	600	100	300
4.	100	200	500	600
5.	50	500	300	

Page 26

1. Tyrone drove 512 miles on a two day trip. ~~He went 55 miles per hour~~. The first day, he drove 305 miles. How may miles did he drive on the second day? 207 miles

2. Vicky worked ~~25 hours~~ last week and earned $175. This week she worked 28 hours and earned $196. How much did she earn altogether? $371

3. ~~There were 271 events in the 1996 Summer Olympic Games~~. The United States won 44 gold, 32 silver, and 25 bronze medals. How many medals did the United States win in all? 101 medals

4. In a vote for favorite ice cream flavor, chocolate got 659 votes. ~~Vanilla got 781 votes, and~~ 246 people voted for strawberry. How many more people voted for chocolate than for strawberry? 413 people

5. One Earth year is about 365 days. One year on Mercury is 88 days. ~~On Mars, a year is 687 days~~. How much shorter is a year on Mercury than on Earth? 277 days

6. A tiger ~~can run 35 miles per hour and~~ sleeps 11 hours a day. A house cat ~~can run 30 miles per hour and~~ sleeps 15 hours a day. How many more hours a day does a house cat sleep than a tiger? 4 hours

7. Kelly's web site got 129 hits on Friday and ~~240 hits on Saturday~~. Tom's web site got 175 hits on Friday ~~and 192 hits on Saturday~~. How many hits did their sites get altogether on Friday? 304 hits

Page 27

	a	b
1.	hundreds	ten thousands
2.	thousands	millions
3.	5 hundreds or 500	3 hundred thousands or 300,000
4.	4 ten thousands or 40,000	6 tens or 60
5.	19,206	
6.	411,035	
7.	2,658,000	
8.	723,104	

	a	b	c
9.	>	=	<

10.	>	<	<
11.	450	270	140
12.	600	400	900
13.	6,000	4,000	9,000

Page 28

	a	b	c	d	e
14.	779	818	562	613	1,032
15.	679	267	901	757	1,104
16.	722	205	164	273	83
17.	731	278	544	512	8
18.	90	1,300	40	300	
19.	200	700	500	1,000	
20.	617	1,398			
21.	48	136			
22.	57	756			

Page 29

23. Ruth: 2,174 runs; Cobb: 2,245 runs; Mays: 2,062 runs

24. Mississippi: 2,348 miles; Yukon: 1,979 miles; Missouri: 2,315 miles

25. There are 100 senators and 435 representatives in Congress. ~~Senators serve 6-year terms and representatives serve 2-year terms~~. How many members are in Congress altogether? 535 members

26. A person who weighs 100 pounds on Earth would weigh ~~254 pounds on Jupiter and~~ 38 pounds on Mars. What is the difference between the weight on Earth and the weight on Mars? 62 pounds

Page 30

	a	b	c	d	e	f
1.	24	14	25	15		
2.	6	16	24	0		
3.	27	16	6	8		
4.	4	12	18	40		
5.	30	15	14	14	9	12
6.	28	40	27	8	9	32
7.	5	20	18	16	45	0

Page 31

	a	b	c	d	e	f
1.	6	12	18	24	30	36
2.	42	48	54	30	18	24
3.	35	56	49			
4.	28	7	42			
5.	0	63	21			

Page 32

	a	b	c	d	e	f
1.	24	32	8	40	48	16
2.	56	72	0	40	56	32
3.	24	72	48	64	8	16
4.	45	54	36			
5.	9	72	0			
6.	81	27	63			

Page 33

	a	b	c	d	e	f
1.	16	12	7	12	72	21
2.	32	8	4	63	40	20
3.	35	54	8	36	6	45
4.	45	18	28	16		
5.	54	42	40	24		

Page 35

1. 20 tiles (4 by 5 grid)
2. 9 panes (3 by 3 grid)
3. 18 servings (6 by 3 grid)
4. 36 chocolates (4 by 9 grid)
5. 56 tulips (7 by 8 grid)

Page 36

	a	b	c	d	e	f
1.	8	4	3	5		
2.	7	8	9	2		
3.	3	1	4	9		
4.	5	6	2	7		
5.	7	1	7	8		
6.	6	8	4	5	1	7
7.	7	2	3	7	9	4
8.	2	6	9	3	1	2

Page 37

	a	b	c	d	e
1.	3	6	8	7	1
2.	4	5	2	9	3
3.	5	4	8	3	
4.	7	1	9	2	

	a	b	c
5.	$7 \times 5 = 35$	$7 \times 3 = 21$	$7 \times 8 = 56$
	$5 \times 7 = 35$	$3 \times 7 = 21$	$8 \times 7 = 56$
	$35 \div 7 = 5$	$21 \div 7 = 3$	$56 \div 8 = 7$
	$35 \div 5 = 7$	$21 \div 3 = 7$	$56 \div 7 = 8$

Page 38

	a	b	c	d	e
1.	6	7	9	4	2
2.	1	8	3	5	6
3.	5	2	4	9	
4.	7	6	3	1	

	a	b	c
5.	$9 \times 5 = 45$	$6 \times 9 = 54$	$3 \times 9 = 27$
	$5 \times 9 = 45$	$9 \times 6 = 54$	$9 \times 3 = 27$
	$45 \div 9 = 5$	$54 \div 9 = 6$	$27 \div 9 = 3$
	$45 \div 5 = 9$	$54 \div 6 = 9$	$27 \div 3 = 9$

Page 40

1. division
8 shells

2. subtraction
448 pages

3. subtraction
134 rats

4. addition
51 dollars

5. multiplication
30 rolls

6. division
4 hours

Page 41

	a	b
1.	4 times 9 is 36.	45 divided by 5 is 9.
	$9 + 9 + 9 + 9 = 36$	$5 \times 9 = 45$, so
	$4 \times 9 = 36$	$45 \div 5 = 9$

	a	b	c	d	e
2.	8	12	9	28	
3.	45	24	56	0	
4.	32	63	18	40	
5.	16	0	7	42	
6.	4	6	27	24	20
7.	36	14	64	0	7
8.	15	81	0	30	72

Page 42

	a	b	c	d	e
9.	9	7	8	7	
10.	9	6	8	8	
11.	8	9	4	8	
12.	6	9	7	6	
13.	7	6	4	4	8
14.	7	8	5	9	4
15.	5	4	4	1	4
16.	5	5	6	6	6

	a	b	c
17.	$6 \times 8 = 48$	$3 \times 8 = 24$	$7 \times 9 = 63$
	$8 \times 6 = 48$	$8 \times 3 = 24$	$9 \times 7 = 63$
	$48 \div 8 = 6$	$24 \div 8 = 3$	$63 \div 9 = 7$
	$48 \div 6 = 8$	$24 \div 3 = 8$	$63 \div 7 = 9$

Page 43

18. 30 stamps
(6 by 5 grid)

19. 64 squares
(8 by 8 grid)

20. multiplication
21 pieces

21. division
5 days

22. subtraction
166 passes

Page 44

	a	b	c	d	e
1.	80	90	50	80	60
2.	55	88	96	54	86
3.	390	840	280	290	990
4.	684	933	486	500	808

Page 45

	a	b	c	d	e
1.	60	48	64	50	84
2.	421	604	366	339	24
3.	66	93	49	88	109
4.	440	609	42	444	23
5.	26	884	900	639	46

	a	b	c
6.	99	480	200
7.	82	55	93

Page 46

	a	b	c	d	e
1.	56	51	96	65	72
2.	168	112	315	156	240
3.	334	852	885	780	777
4.	1,134	1,990	1,185	2,367	3,904

Page 47

	a	b	c	d
1.	812	327	806	909
2.	540	621	812	820
3.	1,227	2,824	4,045	1,010
4.	4,368	2,012	6,132	6,500

Page 49

1. about 100 people
2. about 140 miles
3. about 210 miles
4. about 1,600 movies
5. about 120 dollars

Page 50

	a	b	c	d	e
1.	492	444	540	198	108
2.	4,890	4,218	5,096	1,743	3,500
3.	12,264	15,351	30,632	3,6400	68,880
4.	4,854	1,698	4,470		

Page 51

	a	b	c	d	e
1.	208	384	312	400	536
2.	5,768	4,872	4,212	2,700	6,642
3.	34,263	26,136	37,152	81,459	11,744
4.	2,528	6,424	152		

Page 53

1. $22
2. 216 calories
3. 42 miles
4. 306 flowers
5. 495 pounds

Page 54

	a	b	c	d	e
1.	48	63	150	808	432
2.	450	378	721	1,600	3,164
3.	1,026	500	640	1,530	1,644
4.	15,564	34,560	6,678	27,135	22,856
5.	100	282	288		
6.	166	360	624		
7.	1,799	3,900	11,604		

Page 55

8. yes
9. about 4,500 miles
10. no
11. 176 people
12. 255 dollars

Page 56

	a	b	c
1.	23	14	11
2.	121	42	133

Page 57

	a	b	c
1.	71	54	41
2.	51	30	43
3.	31	52	72

Page 58

	a	b	c
1.	7 R1	8 R3	6 R2
2.	45 R2	56 R1	79 R3
3.	51 R1	69 R2	121 R3

Page 59

	a	b	c
1.	6 R1	9 R2	87
2.	81 R2	20	7 R3
3.	51 R2	7 R1	55 R1
4.	36 R1	6 R1	26
5.	43 R3	8 R1	67
6.	9 R1	39 R1	60 R4

Page 61

1. 4 photographs
2. 3 dimes, 1 penny
3. Jenna is 13 years old, Darius is 8 years old.
4. 4 shirts
5. Adult is $6, child is $3.

Page 62

	a	b	c	d
1.	11	15 R2	3 R6	5 R5
2.	66 R4	72 R2	91 R2	69 R4
3.	711 R2	227 R2	288R1	925

Page 63

	a	b	c	d
1.	4 R7	12 R1	5 R7	2 R2
2.	112 R2	77 R7	51	27
3.	411	138 R7	211	989
4.	12 R1	29 R2	963 R3	
5.	933 R4	62	61 R8	

Page 65

1. 140 pounds **2.** 4,200 feet
3. $175 **4.** 27 weeks
5. 600 inches **6.** 380 books

Page 66

	a	b	c	d
1.	12	21	13 R1	12 R1
2.	47	47	58	41
3.	26	15	54 R5	35 R5
4.	8 R5	5 R8	136 R1	64 R2
5.	32	14 R3	10 R3	
6.	136	148 R7	851 R1	

Page 67

7. 9 books **8.** 7 pies
9. 29 newspapers **10.** $17
11. 55 angelfish

Page 68

	a	b
1.	1 ten ×6 6 tens = 60	4 tens ×8 32 tens =320
2.	3 ×8 24 tens = 240	9 ×1 9 tens = 90
3.	1 hundred ×4 4 hundreds = 400	8 hundreds ×2 16 hundreds = 1,600
4.	7 ×2 hundreds 14 hundreds = 1,400	6 ×3 hundreds 18 hundreds = 1,800

Page 69

	a	b	c	d	e
1.	90	450	350	320	630
2.	540	210	720	180	250
3.	3,600	5,600	1,200	2,700	3,200
4.	3,500	4,200	6,400	2,400	1,800
5.	50	60	70		
6.	100	240	210		
7.	450	350	720		
8.	360	490	480		
9.	1,500	4,800	6,300		
10.	8,100	7,200	4,000		

Page 70

	a	b	c	d
1.	988	990	448	256
2.	585	1,591	572	608
3.	3,975	2,136	3,738	4,672

Page 71

	a	b	c	d	e
1.	924	4,402	1,276	784	4,956
2.	2,116	1,188	504	816	2,997
3.	1,276	544	3,290	1,235	1,175
4.	2,484	1,155	585		
5.	1,116	4,316	935		

Page 72

	a	b	c	d
1.	15,475	28,188	10,579	34,122
2.	10,206	11,480	17,135	19,872
3.	32,402	14,996	23,997	18,668

Page 73

	a	b	c	d	e
1.	20,124	14,681	20,069	15,708	20,174
2.	10,488	4,608	26,048	7,785	8,316
3.	25,536	5,162	4,381	30,240	25,110
4.	17,668	27,115	10,922		
5.	10,428	60,635			

Page 74

	a	b	c	d
1.	600	1,200	900	3,600
2.	2,400	3,600	2,400	4,000
3.	8,000	35,000	42,000	16,000
4.	1,500	4,800	72,000	

Page 75

	a	b	c	d
1.	800	4,200	1,400	1,800
2.	1,600	4,500	6,300	2,000
3.	25,000	36,000	18,000	54,000
4.	32,000	16,000	30,000	56,000
5.	300	3,200	2,400	
6.	20,000	35,000	10,000	

Page 77

1. $1,365 **2.** 1,230 miles
3. 915 people

Page 78

	a	b	c	d
1.	4 R8	7 R2	8	5 R4
2.	9 R7	1	6 R5	2 R3
3.	34	18	20	24
4.	63 R5	72	83 R4	67 R3

Page 79

	a	b	c	d
1.	9 R5	3	3 R2	9 R2
2.	6	7 R3	1 R5	93
3.	5	41	1 R5	2
4.	4 R1	2	3 R6	51
5.	9	7 R3	2	

Page 80

	a	b	c	d
1.	102 R2	307 R1	106 R5	208 R1
2.	40 R4	70 R3	30 R1	50 R3

Page 81

	a	b	c	d
1.	101	109	50 R3	80 R5
2.	60	704 R2	409 R1	90 R7
3.	30 R8	209	304 R1	500
4.	30	700 R4	90	401
5.	40	902	40 R1	

Page 82

	a	b	c
1.	too large	correct	too large
2.	too large	too large	correct
3.	correct	correct	too large

Page 83

	a	b	c
1.	too small	correct	too small
2.	too small	too small	correct
3.	too small	too small	correct

Page 84

	a	b	c	d
1.	13	17 R9	22 R4	26 R7
2.	3 R28	5 R23	8	8 R85
3.	214 R22	326 R9	278 R6	194 R13

Page 85

	a	b	c	d
1.	6 R16	6	58	15 R6
2.	14 R11	19	14 R4	62
3.	76 R27	56	195	126 R22
4.	54	33 R73	35 R59	85 R15
5.	167	29 R47	128 R7	314 R5
6.	11 R72	8 R11	13 R8	
7.	173 R8	202 R26	145 R5	

Page 86

	a	b	c	d
1.	40	50	90	90
2.	700	900	300	700
3.	7	2	20	40
4.	30	60	80	60

Page 87

	a	b	c
1.	90	80	30
2.	50	60	70
3.	500	700	600
4.	90	30	5
5.	8	20	3
6.	200	40	60

Page 89

1. 600 seats **2.** $30
3. 70 times **4.** 3,000 people
5. 9; 9; 90 computers **6.** 3; 3; 30; 300 mph

Page 90

1. 52 miles **2.** 35 boxes
3. $486 **4.** 133 pies
5. about 20 feet **6.** 13 necklaces, 31 left

Page 91

	a	b	c	d
1.	360	280	800	600
2.	578	4,420	1,104	5,963
3.	3,240	16,378	23,374	28,003
4.	1,665	1,292	5,264	
5.	8,668	45,312	21,793	
6.	1,000	2,400	14,000	24,000

Page 92

	a	b	c	d
7.	8 R5	30	2 R9	80 R15
8.	20 R1	110 R4	205 R4	308
9.	5	49	102 R24	62 R40
10.	14 R7	21 R26	53 R75	
11.	too large	too small	correct	
12.	80	700	8	20

Page 93

13. $1,380 **14.** plates
15. 30 times **16.** 7,000 people
17. 80 people

Page 94

	a	b	c	d
1.	4:45	12:30	8:55	7:05

	a	b
2.	2 hours	240 seconds
3.	600 minutes	120 hours
4.	6 days	9 minutes
5.	480 hours	30 minutes

Page 95

	a	b
1.	Wed., Nov. 14, 2001	Tues., March 27, 2001
2.	Tues., Feb. 20, 2001	Wed., July 18, 2001
3.	Wed., Nov. 28, 2001	Thurs., May 31, 2001
4.	168 hours	4 years
5.	21 days	730 days
6.	16 weeks	180 months
7.	156 weeks	12 weeks

Page 96

	a	b
1.	40 minutes	2 hours
2.	3 hrs 25 mins	5 hrs 5 mins
3.	8:25	7:25

Page 97

	a	b
1.	2 hrs 35 mins	1 hr 35 mins
2.	3 hrs 30 mins	1 hr 35 mins
3.	2 hrs 15 mins	1 hr 20 mins
4.	Kansas City	New Orleans
5.	8:00	10:15

Page 98

	a	b
1.	100 pennies	20 nickels
2.	10 dimes	4 quarters
3.	2 half-dollars	5 dollars
4.	10 dollars	3 dimes
5.	11 nickels	5 quarters
6.	$2.30	$7.40
7.	9¢	$10.61
8.	$18.00	$13.02
9.	19¢	90¢

Page 99

	a	b	c	d
1.	$0.56	$0.83	$1.64	$1.81

2.	$7.33	$5.43	$7.60	$36.57
3.	$0.54	$0.13	$1.25	$10.13
4.	$0.49	$0.45	$1.87	$2.78

Page 100

	a	b	c	d
1.	$15.47	$9.28	$22.55	$8.48
2.	$27.50	$29.68	$37.50	$22.77
3.	$0.62	$0.70	$0.50	$0.62
4.	$0.40	$6.00	$6.02	$0.21

Page 102

1. $23.05 **2.** $12.00
3. 5:35 **4.** 2:45
5. $617.06

Page 103

	a	b
1.	in.	ft.
2.	ft.	mi.
3.	lb.	T.
4.	T.	oz.
5.	c.	gal.
6.	c. or pt.	c. or pt.

	a	b	c
7.	32 oz.	1 T.	2 lb.
8.	9 ft.	1 mi.	72 in.
9.	2 qt.	3 pt.	20 qt.

Page 104

	a	b
1.	km	m
2.	m	cm
3.	kg	g
4.	g	kg
5.	mL	mL
6.	L	mL

	a	b	c
7.	3,000 mL	5 m	2,000 g
8.	4,000 m	8 kg	5,000 mL
9.	1,000 cm	6 L	10 m

Page 105

	a	b	c
1.	=	<	>
2.	>	=	=
3.	<	>	<
4.	>	=	<
5.	>	>	<
6.	>	=	=
7.	<	>	=

Page 107

1. African elephant, 7,000 kg
2. American bison, 1,000 kg
3. 2,000 kg
4. 600 kg
5. drinking & eating, 2 gallons
6. bath, 40 gallons
7. 60 gallons
8. 280 gallons

Page 108

	a	b	c	d
1.	6:35	11:45	2:20	4:05

2. 35 days
3. 3 years
4. 420 mins
5. 72 hours
6. 6:55
7. 9:15

8.	$25.06	$9.15		
9.	$5.10	89		
10.	$18.75	$2.84	$75.20	$1.24
11.	>	=		
12.	>	>		

Page 109

	a		b
13.	48 oz.		8,000 lb.
14.	7 yd.		10,560 ft.
15.	4 pt.		5 qt.
16.	2,000 mL		7 m
17.	$178.19	**18.**	7:20

19. rye, 50 loaves **20.** 20 loaves

Page 110

1. 2; $\frac{1}{2}$; one-half
2. 3; $\frac{1}{3}$; one-third
3. 4; $\frac{1}{4}$; one-fourth
4. 5; $\frac{1}{5}$; one-fifth
5. 6; $\frac{1}{6}$; one-sixth
6. 8; $\frac{1}{8}$; one-eighth

Page 111

	a	b
1.	3	6
2.	8	10
3.	5	6
4.	25	7
5.	6	50¢
6.	$2.00	$8.00
7.	$2.00	5

Page 112

	a	b	c
1.	$\frac{7}{9}$	$\frac{6}{7}$	$\frac{3}{8}$
2.	$\frac{4}{5}$	$\frac{9}{10}$	$\frac{8}{9}$
3.	$\frac{2}{3}$	$\frac{7}{8}$	$\frac{5}{7}$
4.	$\frac{5}{9}$	$\frac{2}{7}$	
5.	$\frac{3}{10}$	$\frac{4}{6}$	

Page 113

	a	b	c
1.	$\frac{3}{8}$	$\frac{1}{7}$	$\frac{1}{5}$
2.	$\frac{1}{7}$	$\frac{7}{10}$	$\frac{1}{9}$
3.	$\frac{1}{3}$	$\frac{1}{8}$	$\frac{2}{7}$
4.	$\frac{4}{9}$	$\frac{4}{7}$	
5.	$\frac{3}{10}$	$\frac{1}{8}$	

Page 115

1. 6 choices
2. 4 combinations:
1 quarter, 7 nickels
1 quarter, 5 nickels, 1 dime
1 quarter, 3 nickels, 2 dimes
1 quarter, 1 nickel, 3 dimes
3. 4 sundaes

Page 116

1.
2.
3.
4.

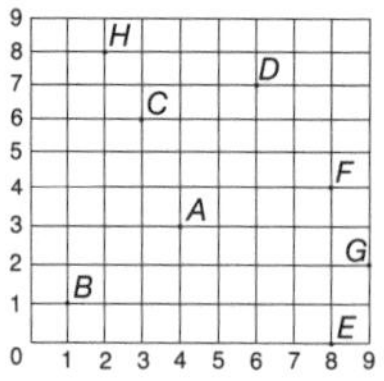

5. (2,7)
6. (5,4)
7. (9,3)
8. (6,1)
9. (0,1)
10. (7,6)
11. (1,4)

Page 117

	a	b	c	d
1.	line segment	ray	line segment	line
2.	$\overline{PQ}$ or $\overline{QP}$	$\overleftrightarrow{BC}$ or $\overleftrightarrow{CB}$	$\overline{JK}$	$\overline{AB}$ or $\overline{BA}$

Possible Answers:
3. $\overrightarrow{PB}$ or ray *PB*
4. $\overleftrightarrow{CB}$ or line *CB*, $\overleftrightarrow{BC}$ or line *BC*
5. $\overline{CP}$ or $\overline{PC}$ or line segment *PQ*
6. *P* or point *P*, *Q* or point *Q*, *C* or point *C*, *B* or point *B*

Page 118

	a	b	c	d
1.	∠*DEF* or ∠*FED*	∠*QRS* or ∠*SRQ*	∠*LMN* or ∠*NML*	∠*EFG* or ∠*GFE*

	a	b	c	d
2.	acute	obtuse	right	acute
3.	right	acute	acute	obtuse

Page 119

	a	b
1.	16 ft	19 yd
2.	27 m	140 in.
3.	40 in.	

Page 120

	a	b
1.	6 square units	8 square units
2.	10 square units	12 square units
3.	16 square units	20 square units

Page 122

1. 288 ft **2.** 240 ft
3. Steve **4.** 2,626 ft
5. 54 ft

Page 123

	a	b	c
1.	4	4	3
2.	18	3	3
3.	$\frac{7}{8}$	$\frac{10}{11}$	$\frac{3}{4}$
4.	$\frac{4}{5}$	$\frac{5}{9}$	$\frac{7}{8}$
5.	$\frac{1}{4}$	$\frac{2}{11}$	$\frac{3}{7}$
6.	$\frac{4}{9}$	$\frac{4}{7}$	$\frac{1}{5}$

7.
8.
9.
10.

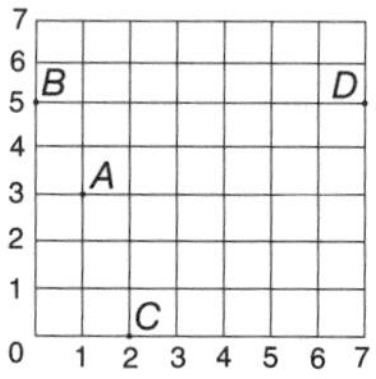

	a	b	c	d
11.	$\overline{AB}$ or $\overline{BA}$	$\overleftrightarrow{PQ}$ or $\overleftrightarrow{QP}$	$\overrightarrow{LM}$	∠*EFG* or ∠*GFE*

Page 124

	a	b	c	d
12.	acute angle	obtuse angle	right angle	obtuse angle

	a	b	c
13.	12 sq. units	8 sq. units	7 sq. units

14. 36 in. **15.** 40 m

16. 9 sandwich choices **17.** 6 different outfits